EXPLORE
 MALTA

D1337852

C016903530

◉ Walking Eye App

Your guide now includes a free eBook to your chosen destination, for the same great price as before. Simply download the Walking Eye App from the App Store or Google Play to access your free eBook.

HOW THE WALKING EYE APP WORKS

Through the Walking Eye App, you can purchase a range of eBooks and destination content. However, when you buy this book, you can download the corresponding eBook for free. Just see below in the grey panel where to find your free content and then scan the QR code at the bottom of this page.

Destinations: Download essential destination content featuring recommended sights and attractions, restaurants, hotels and an A–Z of practical information, all available for purchase.

Ships: Interested in ship reviews? Find independent reviews of river and ocean ships in this section, all available for purchase.

eBooks: You can download your free accompanying digital version of this guide here. You will also find a whole range of other eBooks, all available for purchase.

Free access to travel-related blog articles about different destinations, updated on a daily basis.

HOW THE EBOOKS WORK

The eBooks are provided in EPUB file format. Please note that you will need an eBook reader installed on your device to open the file. Many devices come with this as standard, but you may still need to install one manually from Google Play.

The eBook content is identical to the content in the printed guide.

HOW TO DOWNLOAD THE WALKING EYE APP

1. Download the Walking Eye App from the App Store or Google Play.
2. Open the app and select the scanning function from the main menu.
3. Scan the QR code on this page – you will then be asked a security question to verify ownership of the book.
4. Once this has been verified, you will see your eBook in the purchased ebook section, where you will be able to download it.

Other destination apps and eBooks are available for purchase separately or are free with the purchase of the Insight Guide book.

CONTENTS

ARCHITECTURE

The Knights of St John are famed for making the most architectural impact on Malta. See this for yourself in Valletta (Route 1) and Mdina (Route 7).

RECOMMENDED ROUTES FOR...

BEACHES

The islands have an array of rocky and sandy beaches. The best are in the north of Malta (Route 9) and over on Gozo (Route 11), home to the stunning Ramla Bay.

COASTAL VIEWS

You won't be stuck for gorgeous coastal views, but the best are seen along the Dingli trail (Route 7), over the Grand Harbour from Valletta (Route 1) and from Calypso's Cave in Gozo (Route 11).

ISLAND HOPPERS

The Maltese Archipelago is made up of three main islands. Head to the north of Malta to take the ferry to Comino (Route 12) for a swim in the Blue Lagoon, or across to Gozo (Route 11) for dinner.

MARKETS

Most Maltese towns have a weekly market. The most popular are the daily market on Merchants Street in Valletta (Route 1) and the Sunday fish market in Marsaxlokk (Route 5).

TEMPLES

Seven thousand years of history are showcased here - including the oldest freestanding structures in the world. Head to the Temple Region (Route 4) or over to Gozo (Route 11) to Ggantija.

TOP MUSEUMS

Valletta has been called an 'open air museum' and most of the island's best museums are found here (Route 1), as well as at the Citadel in Gozo (Route 10).

WALKING AND HIKING

Both the north (Route 9) and south (Route 5) of Malta promise fantastic coastal trails for you to follow, while Gozo (Route 11) can be hiked round in a day.

INTRODUCTION

An introduction to Malta's geography, customs and culture, plus illuminating background information on cuisine, history and what to do when you're there.

Traditional houses and walls in Valletta

EXPLORE MALTA

Over 2,000 years have passed since the Ancient Greeks nicknamed the island 'Melitē', meaning 'sweet–honey'. Times have certainly changed since then, but Malta still remains the sweetheart of the Mediterranean.

Located at the crossroads between the Old Continent, the wealthy African mainland and the Near East, Malta has always been at the core of many of history's major events. Yet, while the past is definitely still present in the customs and aesthetics of modern Malta, the country is experiencing a new golden age in business and economy.

GEOGRAPHY

Malta is a tiny island – measuring just 316 sq km and located 93km (57.7 miles) south of Sicily and approximately 300km (186.4 miles) north of Libya, making it one of Europe's most southern points. The archipelago is made up of three inhabited islands, namely Malta, *Ghawdex* (Gozo) and *Kemmuna* (Comino), and another 18 uninhabited islands.

While most of the 18 uninhabited islands are no more than large rocks in the sea, some are of great historical and ecological importance. These include *Hagret il-general* (Fungus Rock) in Dwejra, Gozo, which is one of a handful of places where a para-sitic flowering plant thought to cure dysentery, bleeding and impotence (*Cynomorium Coccineum*) grows. Another is Filfa, which can be spotted from the promenade of Wied iż-Żurrieq, where various species of birds breed on a yearly basis, and an endemic black wall lizard with two tails is said to thrive.

Due to the many hours of strong sunshine experienced in Malta, and the lack of any permanent rivers or lakes, the islands' landscape is characterised by terraced fields, dry vegetation, limestone and rock. And while most woods on the island were cut down centuries ago, olive, fig, citrus, pine, tamarisk and carob trees can be found all across the landscape often grown for their produce.

Malta's most defining geographical feature remains its island-status. It is surrounded by sea on each side, and most beaches on Malta, Gozo and Comino are rocky, with a handful of spectacular sandy beaches located in the north of Malta and on Comino and Gozo, some of the best being Golden Bay, Ramla Bay, Ghajn Tuffieha and St George's Beach.

A boat tour around Gozo inevitably involves a swim in its azure waters

HISTORY AND ARCHITECTURE

The discovery of ancient, free-standing stone structures along the perimeter of Malta and in the heart of Gozo dated Malta's first settlers to 7,000 year ago. Since then, the island has been part of almost every major, Mediterranean civilisation, which includes the Phoenicians, the Carthaginians and the Romans in the ancient world, and the Byzantines, the Arabs, the Normans, the Spanish Aragonese, the Knights of St John, the French and the British in the Common Era.

Its allure throughout the centuries has always remained its strategic location on the Mediterranean trade routes, as well as its natural harbours, but this has often made it a covetable location during times of war, too. Malta, in fact, has picked up many nicknames over the centuries, including 'island fortress' during much of the second millennium and 'the Nurse of the Mediterranean' during World War I.

Malta's role in many wars, but particularly that between the Roman-Catholic West and the Muslim Ottomans, has left Malta a heavily fortified island, boasting tens of watchtowers around the islands' perimeter, as well numerous fortified cities, with Valletta, Mdina, Birgu, Cospicua and Senglea in Malta and Cittadella and Victoria in Gozo being the most noteworthy.

The medieval city of Mdina, which was the capital of the island for many centuries, boasts some of the island's earliest architecture, excluding the temples and the Roman remains scattered across the island. In fact, Malta's real golden age in architecture came with the Knights of St John, who took over the rule of the island in 1530.

Malta's famous baroque (a European architectural style that is characterised by ornate detail) churches and cathedrals were built during the Knights' 250-year period on the island. The current capital city, Valletta, was also built during this time, as were the fortifications surrounding Birgu, all the watchtowers dotting the island and many other important buildings, such as the Sacra Infermeria (the Mediterranean Conference Centre) and the Grandmaster's Palace, both of which are in Valletta. The British also left their mark on the island, building barracks in Pembroke and Mtarfa, among others.

In 1964, Malta became an independent nation state, yet remained part of the British Commonwealth; while 10 years later, in 1974, it became a republic. As of 2004, the country voted to become a Member State of the European Union and, in 2008, it joined the Eurozone.

Today, Malta has become an urbanised island, with numerous hotels and apartment blocks dotting the skyline

Keeping cool

of many of its biggest towns. Yet, the most important architectural occurrence of this century so far remains the Renzo Piano-redesigned entrance to Valletta (City Gate), the new Parliament Building and Pjazza Teatru Rjal theatre (built on the ruins of the Royal Opera House, which was bombed down in World War II).

CLIMATE

Malta is famous for being the island with '300 days of sunshine'. Winters here are mild, with temperatures rarely descending to below 0°C (32°F). Summers can be rather hot however, with the thermometer often registering temperatures of well over 30°C (86°F) in June, July, August and September. Autumn and spring in Malta are also more fluid than in other parts of the continent, with the weather often switching from winter to summer, or vice-versa, in just a few weeks' time.

The annual, average relative humidity in Malta is 73 percent and, coupled with the heat, this makes Malta the ideal place to grow grapes and olives, among other produce. The humidity levels normally go down to an average of 65 percent during the summer months and up to 78 percent during the winter months.

The high temperatures in summer may be too hot to handle for senior citizens and young children, and mid-May to mid-June and mid-October to mid-November tend to be the best months to visit. For those looking to sunbathe, then July and August are the best months but, be warned, it may be too hot to do much else.

POPULATION

Malta has a population of around 460,000 people, of which around 10 percent are non-Maltese. Each year, the island also welcomes an average of 1.5 million tourists, which, considering its size, makes it very densely populated.

Most nationals identify as Roman Catholics, and the 360 churches on Malta, Gozo and Comino, along with the numerous Religious holidays celebrated here, attest to that. Even so, there are thriving Protestant, Muslim, Jewish and Buddhist communities, among others.

Since the 1970s, many expats from the United Kingdom have moved here, and they have been joined by many Scandinavians and northern Europeans who relocated here due to the recent boom in the iGaming and financial services industries.

The island, particularly in places like St Julian's, Sliema and Valletta, is cosmopolitan and multicultural; not just in its people, but also in the variety of shops, restaurants and businesses found there.

Maltese nationals pride themselves in being welcoming and giv-

The manicured Upper Barrakka Gardens

ing, so don't be shocked if you ask for directions and you're led by the hand to your destination.

Family

Family remains the most important part of life in Malta and, for the majority of the population, getting married and having children remains a priority. Most young men and women will find a spouse from within their village or extended community, and big, lavish wedding ceremonies are the order of the day, flamboyantly celebrating the start of a new couple's life together.

Regular family events are also the norm. Most Maltese are never happier than when sitting around a large table and enjoying a sumptuous meal with their relatives. The old, young and very

DON'T LEAVE MALTA WITHOUT...

Trying a Maxokk ftira. An icon among locals, the Maxokk ftira (Gozo's answer to pizza) can be purchased from a tiny bakery, called Maxokk, in Nadur, Gozo (www.maxokkbakery.com).

Going to the Upper Barrakka. As one of British Malta's ultimate monuments, the Upper Barrakka Gardens in Valletta have the best view of the majestic Grand Harbour. See page 37.

Having *te fit-tazza*. Visit a village bar or band club and ask for tea served in a glass. It's an age-old tradition here, and even the young have taken it up as the next cool thing, particularly after a night out.

Indulging in *pastizzi*. Along with your *te fit-tazza* sink your teeth into some delicious *pastizzi* (diamond-shaped pastry cases typically stuffed with peas or ricotta). See page 18.

Visiting a *festa*. Every village in Malta has at least one patron saint, and the whole village gets together once a year to commemorate their patron saint's achievements. These mostly take place in summer, and it's best to visit www.visitmalta.com to discover when the next one is on. See page 38.

Attending the Birgu flea market. From World War II memorabilia to vintage toys and old knick-knacks, the Sunday morning Birgu flea market (on Triq San Dwardu, Birgu) is the ultimate haunt for collectors and antiquarians. See page 43.

Visiting the Blue Lagoon. Located on the island of Comino, almost every local and foreigner who's ever visited this spot will claim it as one of the most striking beaches anywhere in the world. See page 82.

Stepping foot into St John's Co-Cathedral. The Knights of St John's ultimate present to God and Country was the lavish, gilded and marbled interior of St John's Co-Cathedral. The floor has been dubbed 'the most beautiful in the world', and no one has come forth to challenge that, yet! See page 32.

young muddle together, relishing each other's company and sharing stories. There remains a genuine respect for the family's elders and their wisdom, and it is still common for the *nanna* or *nannu* to reside with the younger generations into their retirement.

Local pace

The pace of life of the Maltese is rarely straightforward. The major towns and cities are a hub for commerce, welcoming office workers, shoppers and commuters every day of the week. The villages, however, remain calm and peaceful, with mostly local shops and churches driving the daily grind. Siesta, while still practised in certain parts of the island (noon to 1pm–3 to 4pm), is mostly a thing of the past in most cities and towns.

In summer, evenings can be spent at seaside towns and villages where restaurants, bars and clubs cater to locals and tourists. The party-mile in St Julian's, known as Paceville, is by far the most popular, with hundreds of partygoers descending onto the bars in the area, particularly on Mondays, Wednesdays, Fridays, Saturdays and Sundays. Sliema and Valletta are favoured by people looking for a relaxed drink, dinner or pleasant walk. And these remain as popular in the winter months.

Paceville, however, tends not to be as busy or crowded during the week in winter, with Fridays and Saturdays being the biggest nights of the week. Same goes for the wine bars, particularly in villages at the centre of Malta, namely Attard, Naxxar, Lija and Birkirkara, as well as in the Three Cities.

Most museums in Malta close at 5pm in both summer and winter, with last admission being at 4.30pm. Between March and December, however, Heritage Malta sites (www.heritagemalta.org) close at 6pm, with the last admission being 5.30pm.

POLITICS AND ECONOMICS

Malta's political scene is made up of three main political parties, the *Partit Laburista* (the Labour Party), the *Partit Nazzjonalista* (the Nationalist Party) and the *Alternattiva Demokratika* (the Greens). The Labour Party, which is technically centre-left, was re-elected into government in March 2017, repeating their 2013 victory which followed almost 25 years of Nationalist leadership. Economically and politically speaking, Malta is a stable country despite its lack in natural mineral resources; the country relies heavily on tourism.

Malta is also a Member State of the European Union (since 2004), part of the Eurozone (since 2008) and part of the Schengen Agreement (since 2007). Some 51 years after gaining Independence in 1974, Malta is still part of the Commonwealth of Nations (of which it became an independent

Sandy Ramla Bay, on Malta's northern coast

state in 1964). It is also a Member State of the Union for the Mediterranean (since it was founded in 2008) and the United Nations (since 1964).

TOP TIPS FOR EXPLORING MALTA

Hop-on, hop-off. Hop-on, hop-off Malta Bus Tours run two different routes in Malta: the Red Route, which goes to the south, and the Blue Route, which heads to the north, and there's also the Gozo Green Route. All buses stop at most landmarks around the island, and are well worth the money. Visit www.getyourguide.com or www.maltasightseeing.com for more information.

The Hypogeum. Dating back almost 5,000 years, the Hypogeum of Hal-Saflieni is one of the oldest underground buildings in the world. Tickets sell out really quickly and it's fully-booked for months, so make sure to reserve yours on www.heritagemalta.org as soon as you can.

Handling the heat. With temperatures sometimes exceeding 40°C (104°F) during the summer months, it's important to be prepared. Sun cream is essential whether you're going to the beach or out for a day of shopping or sightseeing; and so is a hat, a fan and a bottle of cold water. If you're hitting the beach, an umbrella won't go amiss, either.

Mosquitoes. Make sure you have an insect-repelling spray handy as many people report being bitten by mosquitoes and tiger mosquitoes throughout the year. If you get bitten, apply surgical spirit to the bite to stop it from itching. If it gets infected, visit a pharmacist.

Getting into churches. Most churches will not let you enter their premises unless you're wearing appropriate clothing. Shorts are generally accepted so long as they are not too short. Tank tops aren't, so make sure you carry a shawl with you if you're planning on visiting any.

Getting around. A single journey on a bus costs €1.50 in winter, €2 in summer and €3 at night, but you can get a Tallinja Card Explore for €21 (adults) or €15 (children), which entitles you to seven days of unlimited travel, including night services.

Sundays. Most shops are closed on Sundays, including supermarkets; but you will find a number of places open in St Julian's. For a list of pharmacies open on that particular Sunday, please consult that day's edition of *The Times of Malta on Sunday* (www.timesofmalta.com). The pharmacy at the Malta International Airport is usually open every Sunday.

Tipping. Tipping your waiter is a common custom in Malta, although it is not enforced. The typical amount is 10 percent of the total – unless a service charge is automatically added. Tipping taxi drivers, hairdressers, masseurs, etc. is not required but obviously welcomed.

Rabbit stew, Malta's national dish

FOOD AND DRINK

The 300 days of sunshine enjoyed yearly by the islanders is also the backbone for Malta's tasty produce. This, in turn, is used in age-old recipes that marry Mediterranean and continental cuisine, as well as in the delicious array of wines made locally.

Malta's cuisine is akin to its language, in that they both have a solid base in the island's history and the cultures that once dominated its people. Many of Malta's best-loved recipes are incredibly similar to those of other nations, including Sicily, Italy, England and Greece. The island is not just known for its grub, but also for its wine, with production dating back some 2,000 years.

Unlike some other cuisines, however, Maltese food isn't meant to be refined or light, but rather nourishing and hearty. In fact, if you get to dine with a local family, expect large portions of everything and second helpings, as the mark of a good host is making sure that his or her guest leaves feeling very, very full.

LOCAL CUISINE

The Maltese diet tends to be very heavy on the carbs, with pasta, pastry and potatoes making it into many local dishes; and these are often combined with meats.

Rabbit stew, which usually includes potatoes, is often served with spaghetti; while rabbit meat is served with chips. Rigatoni Bolognese, on the other hand, is often encased in pastry and baked. Horsemeat and quail are also considered local delicacies which often come with a side of vegetables and roasted potatoes or chips.

Fish is another staple of the Maltese cuisine, with many seasonal and year-round types of fish grilled, fried and stewed into some of the island's favourite recipes. The local favourite is the *lampuki* (dorado; mahi-mahi).

Different parts of Malta are renowned for different things. Marsaxlokk and the surrounding areas are celebrated for their fish restaurants; while Imgarr is the best place for a *fenkata* (rabbit feast), where you'll get to try *bebbux* (snails), *summien* (quail), *hobż biż-żejt* (Maltese bread with tomatoes, olive oil, capers and olives), *stuffat tal-fenek* (rabbit stew) and *fenek moqli* (fried rabbit).

Over the past couple of years, the island has also seen a rise in restaurants serving organic and locally-sourced foods; and many of them now have at least one vegetarian or vegan item on the menu.

The de Mondion Restaurant

Għejnas, peppered cheeselets

WHERE TO EAT

Although most eateries do not tend to be segregated into different categories (such as restaurants, brasseries, etc.) by the locals, there is still a mix of places you can dine at.

Local restaurants

Many restaurants in Malta serve at least one traditional dish, but there are some that specialise in the local cuisine. Ta' Kris in Sliema, Gululu in St Julian's (see page 40) and Dar il-Bniet in-Dingli (see page 64) have the best reputations. The décor also tends to be reminiscent of a Malta that has been lost to time.

Foreign restaurants

Foreign cuisine has become all the rage over the past decade, with Asian, Italian, Lebanese and Japanese restaurants now located all over the island.

Eastern restaurants dot the streets of many towns in Malta, but the most popular remain those in St Julian's. Some of Malta's top five-star hotels also have their own Asian restaurants, including the Hilton Hotel (The Blue Elephant; see page 96) and the Corinthia Palace Hotel & Spa (Rickshaw; see page 99).

The most popular Lebanese on the island is Ali Baba in Gżira, and their *Inghatt Agel* (traditionally prepared veal brains with lemon juice and sumac) are one of the more unusual-yet-sought-after specialities.

Japanese restaurants have also caught on, with Zest (see page 97), Zen Sushi and SushiBa being just a few you should try out.

Pizzerias

The term 'restaurant' in Malta is an all-encompassing one, and includes what the Italians would refer to as a *trattoria* or a *pizzeria*, and most restaurants have a mixed menu that includes fish, pasta, meats, pizza and soups. Even the more specialised establishments,

---

Local sweets

While every season comes with its own, unique sweets, there are various special treats you can buy all year round.

Honey rings (*Qagħaq ta' l-Għasel*) are one such local delicacy. These pastry tubes are filled with black treacle, marmalade, orange peel, spices and honey, and have become a symbol of Malta in their own right. They can be purchased from Caffè Cordina at 244, Republic Street, Valletta, among other places.

Imqaret (deep-fried, date-stuffed pastry cases) are also a favourite, and you'll find Malta's most famous seller outside Valletta's City Gate on the left-hand side, nestled amid the many permanent stalls there.

Biskuttini tar-raħal (village biscuits) and *biskuttini tal-lewż* (almond biscuits) are also available at most confectionaries around the island.

A selection of local liqueurs, including the deliciously sweet bajtra

such as Marsaxlokk's fish restaurants, tend to have at least one meat dish, one vegetarian dish, and, most probably, a pizza or two.

If it's just a good pizza you're after however, head to Vecchia Napoli (see page 98) in Sliema and Sky Parks, La Cuccagna in Sliema, Il Mandraggio in Valletta and Ir-Rokna in St Julian's.

Cafés

Cafés all over the island, but particularly in Valletta, Sliema and St Julian's, serve sandwiches and snacks throughout the day, with some also having pasta or meat dishes on offer for lunch and early dinner. These are usually open from 7–9am until 7pm.

Pastizzerias

While you'll find most international fast-food chains in Malta, the islanders' fast-food of choice remains the humble *pastizz* (a diamond-shaped pastry case stuffed primarily with mushy peas or ricotta). Many cafés and village bars serve them, but the locals prefer buying them from *pastizzerias*, which are usually small hole-in-the-wall shops. Located all over the island – sometimes, in the most unlikely of places – they sell an array of foods, including *timpana* (penne Bolognese encased in pastry), a variety of pies, *qassatati* (a cross between a *pastizz* and a pie), pizza, chicken *pastizzi*, sausage rolls and apple pies.

Bars

Many bars now tend to have a Happy Hour on an almost-daily basis, and many of them also serve nibbles, snacks or tapas. The Italian *aperitivo* is also starting to catch on, with a number of bars and restaurants in Valletta seeing an influx of office workers, lawyers and shoppers heading there for a quick drink after a long day's work.

DRINKS

Malta's two favourite tipples remain beer and wine, and the islanders are proud of the ones they produce themselves.

Cisk

The island's most famous, locally-produced beer remains the Cisk (www.cisk.com) and its multiple variants (Cisk Chill, Cisk Excel, Cisk Export, and Cisk Strong). Pronounced 'Chisk', the name is believed to have been derived from a mispronunciation of the word 'cheque', and has been brewed on the island since 1929. The brand is part of one of Malta's largest companies, Simonds Farsons Cisk Plc. The original Cisk lager can be found virtually everywhere on the island, and it's probably more ubiquitous than Coca-Cola.

Wine

Production of wine in Malta dates back to the times of the Phoenicians, who ruled the island over 2,000 years ago.

The two major wineries are Marsovin and Delicata

This is hardly surprising as the island's unique climate produces some delicious grape varieties, including the two indigenous ones, the *Gellewża* and the *Ghirghentina*.

The first local, commercially produced wines appeared in the 20th century, when Marsovin (www.marsovin.com) and Emmanuel Delicata (www.delicata.com) first opened their doors. By the 1970s, many foreign grape varieties were being planted, which include Cabernet Sauvignon, Sauvignon Blanc, Syrah, Merlot, Chardonnay, Carignan, Chenin Blanc, Grenache and Moscato. In the 2000s, Meridiana (www.meridiana.com.mt), Camilleri Wines and Montekristo (www.montekristo.com) joined the industry.

Undoubtedly, Malta's hot and humid climate is one of the key factors in grape harvesting on the island. Grapes here ripen much quicker than in other countries further north, and the mix of limestone terroir and sea salt sprayed by the sea and carried by the winds all add up to give the grapes their particular and unique taste.

While Maltese wines may not be as renowned as those of Malta's neighbours, such as Italy or France, they have, over the years, won many international medals and accolades abroad.

Kinnie

Made from a mixture of orange flavouring and aromatic herbs, Kinnie (www.kinnie.com) is probably the island's favourite soft drink. It was first launched by Farsons in 1952, with the diet version introduced in 1984, the zero-sugar version (Kinnie Zest) in 2007, and the naturally-sweeted version (Kinnie Vita) in 2014. Opinions are divided about Kinnie, with some locals hailing it as the best soft drink out there, and others who loathe its slightly-bitter taste. Whatever your palate, no trip to Malta would be complete without at least trying it.

Bajtra liqueur

The *Opuntia ficus-indica*, more commonly known as the prickly pear or, in Maltese, *bajtra*, was first introduced to the Mediterranean from the Americas at the end of the 15th century. Since then, it has become a quintessential Maltese fruit, flourishing in the wild amid the rubble-walls and forgotten pathways.

Zeppi's Bajtra Liqueur is made from this particular fruit, which is a member of the Cactus family, and is deliciously sweet. It can be drunk chilled or on ice, or, for a delicious cocktail, try it with champagne.

Food and drink prices

Throughout this book, price guide for a three-course à la carte dinner for one with a bottle of house wine:
€€€€ = over 60 euros
€€€ = 40–60 euros
€€= 25–40 euros
€ = below 25 euros

Lace maker at work

SHOPPING

In recent years, Malta's shopping scene has exploded, bringing with it numerous flagships and designer brands, artisanal markets and speciality shops.

Up until a few years ago, shoppers in Malta were constrained to tiny boutique shops in village squares and a handful of foreign brands that had been brought to the island. Today, it's a completely different story, with new shopping complexes opening on an almost-yearly basis, a thriving crafts village and several shopping centres located on both Malta and Gozo.

ANTIQUES

The Birgu Flea Market, which takes place every Tuesday between 7am–noon on Triq San Dwardu in Birgu, is reminiscent of those in Paris and London. You'll find everything here: from old photographs to vintage toys, World War II memorabilia and out-of-print books. Make sure to go as early as possible as all the best pieces are snatched up quickly.

CRAFTS

The Ta' Qali Crafts Village in Ta' Qali is the ultimate destination for shoppers looking for genuine, hand-made, Maltese crafts. Tours of various factories are also available, and you'll be able to see craftsmen blowing glass, creating items using silver filigree, and even working on lace. This is the perfect spot to purchase a special souvenir however, the site is currently undergoing renovation so the number of places open may vary.

FASHION

Malta has a number of shopping complexes where you can find many international labels side-by-side. These include The Point (www.thepointmalta.com) and The Plaza (www.plaza-shopping.com) in Sliema, Baystreet (www.baystreet.com.mt) in St Julian's, Main Street (www.mainstreetcomplex.com) in Paola, Daniels Shopping & Residential Complex in Hamrun, Arkadia (www.arkadia.com.mt) and The Duke (www.thedukegozo.com) in Victoria, Gozo, and Pama Shopping Village in Mosta.

Various towns around Malta and Gozo are renowned for their concentration of shops on their high streets, including Sliema, St Julian's, Valletta, Paola, amrun, Mosta and Victoria in Gozo.

Filigree, a Maltese speciality

Maltese glassware

Local designer goods can be found at the Charles & Ron's boutique shop at the Corinthia Palace Hotel & Spa (www.corinthia.com/palace), camilleriparismode (www.camilleriparismode.com) and Henri (www.henri.com.mt) in Mdina, among others.

FILIGREE

The Maltese Islands have a long tradition of filigree-making, and today Malta is one of the few countries where this craft is still widely practiced. Filigree is made by melting silver or gold to produce ingots. These are then pressed and stretched several times to create wires. The wires are then bent and shaped into various jewellery items. You can find these in various jewellery shops around the island, particularly those in Mdina.

FOOD & WINE

The Maltese love their food, and you'll be sure to find various cafés and speciality shops selling an assortment of Maltese delicacies. From honey rings to nougat, special coffee blends to sea salt, and preserves to olive oil, there's something to tickle everyone's fancy. Seasonal sweets include *prinjolata* and *perlini* at Carnival, which takes place around 40 days before Easter, and *figolli* (almond cakes) at Easter time.

Local wines range from sweet, white wines like moscato to intense reds, like merlot. Wine tasting can be done at various estates and wine bars around the island.

GLASS

Although the first glass-blowing factory opened its doors in 1968, glass blowing in Malta has really caught on and is now considered one of the most important crafts on the island. There are various companies making glassware, most notably Mdina Glass (www.mdinaglass.com.mt), Phoenician Glass and Valletta Glass (www.vallettaglass.com).

Items here range from vases to paperweights and jewellery to Christmas ornaments and, while fragile, they make for the perfect souvenir to take home.

Shopping hours

Opening times are typically from 9 or 10am–7pm at most shopping centres. Certain shopping complexes, however, have their own opening hours, including The Point at Tigné Point in Sliema (Mon–Sat 10am–7.30pm, Sun 11am–6.30pm) and Baystreet, St Julian's (daily 10am–10pm). Some local shops, mostly those located in the village cores, tend to close between noon, 1–3 or 4pm and are closed on Saturday afternoons and all day on Sundays.

The annual Isle of MTV in full swing

ENTERTAINMENT

Embrace Malta's budding cultural scene with weekly theatrical productions, dance shows, concerts and art exhibitions. Alternatively, at the weekends, head over to one of the many bars offering live music and homemade wines.

Valletta is Malta's cultural capital city, with the Manoel Theatre (www.teatru-manoel.com.mt), the Renzo Piano-designed Pjazza Teatru Rjal (www.pjazzateatrurjal.com) and St James Cavalier Centre for Creativity (www.sjcav.org) all located within the perimeter of the city.

Valletta is also rekindling its once-legendary nightlife; but St Julian's and Sliema remain the ultimate late-night hot spots with their plethora of clubs, bars, restaurants and pubs.

THEATRE

Considering Malta's size, it boasts an impressive number of theatres. Most of them are to be found in Valletta, including Europe's oldest working theatre, the Manoel Theatre.

The local theatre season usually opens in October and closes in May, and it's as varied as they come: comedies, dramas, Shakespearean plays, Broadway-favourites or alternative theatre. The best place to check what's on when you're in Malta is the Malta Tourism Authority's official What's On section at www.visitmalta.com.

DANCE

Thanks to the ŻfinMalta Dance Ensemble (www.zfinmalta.org), Malta's national dance company, dance has become an integral part of Malta's cultural scene. Each season, a number of contemporary and interdisciplinary shows are produced at various theatres, including the Manoel Theatre and Pjazza Teatru Rjal. Full-length ballets, although a rarity in Malta, are produced sporadically.

MUSIC

Music takes many guises in Malta. At one extreme, you can experience the unique sound of *Ghana* (Maltese folk music) at the Ghanafest, which normally takes place in June. At the other, every June (or July) Malta hosts The Isle of MTV: Malta Special, where various famous artists fly to Malta for a one-off concert that is free to the public. Past acts have included Lady Gaga, Enrique Iglesias, Kelis, The Black-Eyed Peas, Jason Derulo and Rita Ora.

Some bars and restaurants, particularly in Valletta, also have bands and

A performance at the Manoel Theatre

musicians playing live on Fridays and Saturdays, often next to the terrace tables in the summer.

Opera on Gozo

Gozo has a thriving operatic scene, with its two main theatres, the Astra and the Aurora, located on Triq ir-Repubblika in Victoria. Each year in October, both theatres present an operatic production for a number of nights (or, sometimes, just for one night) and tickets sell incredibly fast.

FILM

Malta has been the backdrop for many major Hollywood blockbusters and famous TV shows. Films include *Midnight Express* (1978), *Troy* (2004), *Munich* (2005), *Agora* (2009), *Captain Phillips* (2013), *By the Sea* (2015) and TV-wise, the ever-popular *Game of Thrones* is partly filmed on the islands.

Surprisingly enough, the film that has left the most impact on the island was the 1980 live-action adaptation of *Popeye*, starring the late Robin Williams. The set, which was a specially constructed village at the edge of Mellieha, was turned into the Popeye Village theme park (www.popeyemalta.com).

NIGHTLIFE

No matter where you're based, nightlife in Malta is never too far away. Valletta is by far the most buzzing with theatrical events, concerts and art exhibitions; and places like Strait Street and Pjazza San Gorg now have a thriving bar scene.

St Julian's, with its party-mile Paceville, remains the capital of late-night entertainment with venues such as the SO City Club and the Footloose Fun Bar being two popular options. Its neighbour Sliema, on the other hand, is perfect for a quiet drink or a dinner overlooking the Marsamxett Harbour, with views stretching all the way to Valletta's imposing bastions.

The islands also boast plenty of bars and restaurants, mostly in the city centre. Gozo in particular has an incredible party scene, most notably at La Grotta, a venue that attracts some of the best international DJs.

FESTIVALS

Malta's cultural calendar is peppered with festivals. January kicks off with two weeks of classical music during The Valletta Baroque Festival (www.vallettabaroquefestival.com.mt). Summer is jam-packed with the Valletta Film Festival (www.vallettafilmfestival.com) in June, Malta Arts Festival (www.maltaartsfestival.org) in June and July, the Malta Jazz Festival (www.maltajazzfestival.org) in July, and Kinemastik Film Festival (www.kinemastik.org) and two wine festivals in July/August. Between October and December, there is also the Festival Mediterranea (www.mediterranea.com.mt), with operas, art exhibitions and classical concerts closing off the year.

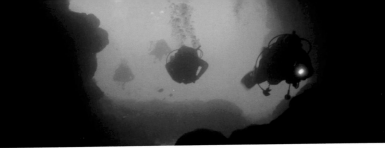

Diving into the Santa Maria Caves, on the northern shore of Comino island

OUTDOOR ACTIVITIES

Malta is one of the Mediterranean's top up-and-coming destinations for outdoor pursuits, boasting some of the world's most stunning diving spots, hidden pockets of untouched countryside and a state-of-the-art golf course.

While beaches remain the ultimate attraction for active visitors, there are many other pursuits you can try. For years, Malta and Gozo have been voted among the best diving destinations in the world by readers of various websites and magazines, and, although the island may seem mostly urbanised, there are still many places you can go to for long walks.

BEACHES

When it comes to beaches, Malta's map is divided into two: sandy beaches in the north and rocky beaches in the south – with a handful of exceptions scattered along the way. Mellieha Bay and Golden Bay in Malta and Ramla Bay in Gozo are by far the most popular with families. For something more secluded, try San Blas in Gozo or St Peter's Pool in the south of Malta.

The Blue Lagoon in Comino is also a firm favourite, but if you decide to venture here make sure you go as early as possible as hundreds of people descend onto the tiny, sandy beach by 11am. The ferry to Comino leaves from Cirkewwa in the north.

DIVING AND SNORKELLING

Malta, Gozo and Comino's coasts have a wealth of aquatic flora and fauna, so snorkelling and diving here is a real feast for the eyes. The Blue Hole in Dwejra, Gozo, is among the most spectacular as you will swim through a large vertical crack in the reef and over the ruins of the Azure Window. At the other side of the channel, the P29 dive in Cirkewwa also allows divers to explore the wreck of a German Kondo class minesweeper.

Most of Malta's diving sites are suitable to all levels, but if you're not qualified or confident enough, or if you've never dived before, there are a number of diving schools to guide you in both Malta and Gozo. The Sliema Front tends to be one of the best places to source one of these.

WATER SPORTS

Mellieha in the north is the best place to learn how to windsurf and water ski. Parasailing fans should head to Golden Bay, for a bird's-eye view of Malta's fascinating northwestern tip

The pristine greens of the Royal Malta Golf Club

and striking views across to Comino and Gozo.

TREKKING

When you first land on Malta, you may assume that the whole country is one, large urbanised area – but this is a mistake even many of the locals make. Venturing out of the towns and villages, you will quickly discover a completely different island, with flora and fauna you never expected to see.

Dingli Cliffs and Bahrija in the east are some of the best places to go trekking, away from the commotion of city life. That said, with Malta being so small, you'll never be too far away from a main road or a bus stop. Also consider an excursion to Buskett Gardens, a tiny stretch of woods – the last on the whole archipelago – where you'll find some of the island's endemic plants, trees and fungi.

GOLF

The Marsa Sports Club houses the Royal Malta Golf Club and its 18-hole golf course laid out amid lush swathes of grass and trees. The modern clubhouse also has a well-stocked Pro Shop, changing facilities, and an indoor bar and restaurant which is used in the winter months. Regular clubs can be leased out for €25, elite clubs for €35, pull trolleys for €5 and electric buggies for €38. Dress code and proper etiquette are given the utmost importance at the club. For more information and to book a green fee go to www.royalmaltagolf-club.com.

Top diving sites

Whether you're a seasoned scuba diver or are still finding your flippers, the Maltese Islands promise a huge variety of dive sites that are bound to entice you into the water. Depending on your abilities, this is our pick of the must-see spots below the surface:

Cirkewwa. Easily the island's most popular dive site, this whole area is marine-protected. Keep your eyes peeled for barracudas, jacks and tuna.

Um el-Faroud. This wreck was sunk following a tragic accident in 1995, and now sits off the southern village of Zurrieq. Only recommended for experienced divers.

Ghar Lapsi. Great for divers of all abilities, immerse yourself among caverns, reefs and caves, and enjoy plenty of typical Mediterranean marine fauna.

Dwejra Point, Gozo. This area's unique limestone formations make it a must for any diver. The water visibility here is probably the best on the island.

Le Polynésien. Nicknamed 'Malta's *Titanic*', this is the wreck of a 19th-century passenger liner that sank at the end of World War I. Tech divers only.

Ggantija Temples on Gozo

HISTORY: KEY DATES

Malta's geographical location has made it a covetable asset for centuries, from the Knights of St John, British occupation to its siege during World War II. It is now an independent nation very much looking to the future.

EARLY HISTORY

Pre-5million BC	Malta is part of landmass joining Europe to Africa.
5000 BC	Neolithic Age: Red and Grey Skorba period; temple of Ta' Hagrat is built.
4000–3000 BC	The Copper Age: Megalithic temples built at Ggantija (Gozo), Tarxien, Hagar Qim and Mnajdra.
2500–900 BC	The Bronze Age: Borg in-Nadur inhabited. The Hypogeum Burial Chamber excavated over a period of 500 years.
675–600 BC	Phoenician colonisation of the islands.
480 BC	Carthaginian domination.
264 BC	First Punic War.

ROMAN & MEDIEVAL MALTA

218 BC	Malta incorporated into the Republic of Rome.
AD 60	St Paul converts Malta's Governor Publius to Christianity.
330	Byzantine rule begins.
533	Belisarius, Justinian's general, establishes a port on Malta.
870	The Aghlabid Caliphs conquer the island.
1091	The Normans land on the island; Count Roger of Sicily force out the Arabs.
1266–83	The Angevin dynasty rules.
1283–1530	The Spanish Aragonese dominate life on Malta.
1350	King Ludwig of Sicily establishes the Maltese nobility.

THE KNIGHTS OF ST JOHN & BRITISH RULE

1530	The Order of St John takes possession of the islands.
1551	Gozo attacked by Ottoman forces, who are repelled after a prolonged battle.

The destructive aftermath of an Axis aerial bombardment in Senglea

1561	The Inquisition is established.
1565	The Great Siege of Malta is won by the Knights.
1566	Founding of Valletta.
1798	Napoleon conquers Malta; the Order of St John leaves the island and the Inquisition is abolished.
1799	The Maltese rise against French domination. Britain offers its protection. French forces surrender one year later.
1802	Maltese Declaration of Rights asks that the islands come under the protection of the British Crown.
1814	Treaty of Paris; Malta becomes a British Crown Colony.
1914–18	World War I: A destination for wounded troops, Malta is known as the 'Nurse of the Mediterranean'.
1921	Granted self-government over domestic affairs; the first Maltese parliament is convened.
1940	First Maltese civilian casualties of World War II – killed by air raids.
1942	Second Great Siege; Britain awards the islands the George Cross.
1947	Self-government is restored.

MODERN MALTA

1964	Malta becomes an independent state within the British Commonwealth.
1972	An agreement is signed with Britain and Nato allowing the use of the islands as a military base.
1974	Malta becomes a republic, but remains part of the Commonwealth.
1979	Last British forces leave.
1992	Queen Elizabeth II visits the islands where she dedicates the World War II Siege Bell Memorial.
1998	Nationalists regain power, led by Dr Eddie Fenech Adami.
2001	Pope John Paul II visits Malta to beatify the first Maltese saints of the Roman Catholic Church.
2004	Malta joins the EU.
2008	Malta adopts the euro as its currency.
2015	New parliament building by Renzo Piano opens in Valletta.
2017	Malta takes up EU presidency. The Azure Window collapses.
2018	Valletta is the European Capital of Culture.
2019	Sixteen- and seventeen-year-olds vote for the first time in the EU Parliament elections.

BEST ROUTES

VALLETTA

Malta's Unesco World Heritage capital has been given a much-needed facelift in recent years, effectively combining its incredible history and architecture with a more cosmopolitan approach. This is the place on Malta for dining, culture, history and shopping.

DISTANCE: 8km (4.3 miles)
TIME: Full day
START: City Gate
END: City Gate
POINTS TO NOTE: Getting to the capital is easy, as almost all buses end up here at some point on their route. It is also easy to walk around the capital at a pace that suits, and the time needed here will depend on how many museums and attractions you want to visit. If you really want to enjoy the city in depth, then this itinerary could be spread over two days.

Visitors to Valletta a few decades ago may remember a bustling and commercial capital city (but arguably not very chic). It was always the capital of business and commerce, but it had lost a lot of its lustre in World War II and hadn't quite recovered.

Today, though, all that has changed. Malta's Baroque capital has undergone a complete transformation, converting it into a modern city that has many roles to play – from commercial centre and business hub, to tourist destination and cultural nucleus. It has become the city that so many dreamed it could be.

CITY GATE

This is probably where you will see the starkest transformation, and notice the most modern architecture that the city has to offer.

Before you walk across the bridge before you, note the former moat below. Dug by Turkish slaves, and measuring 17 metres (55ft) deep by 9 metres (29ft) wide, the moat extends for 875 metres (2,840ft) between the two harbours.

As you walk into the **City Gate ❶**, leaving the busy bus terminal and Triton's Fountain behind you, you will be dazzled by the new Renzo Piano-designed **Parliament Building** on your right. This is the project that has truly given Valletta its new lease of life. It took five years to complete, cost over €90 million to build and was officially inaugurated in May 2015, effectively kick-starting a new phase in Valletta's

Valletta at dusk

history. The **City Gate Steps** to the left and the right of the City Gate Bridge now connect this part of the city to the top of the Bastions, and to St James' Cavalier and St John's Cavalier.

Further along the road is **Pjazza Teatru Rjal** (www.pjazzateatrurjal.com), the transformed Old Opera House that was extensively bombed in World War II. This project caused a great deal of con-

troversy as the team behind it chose to make it an open-air theatre around the bombed ruins instead of restoring the opera house to its former glory, much to the dismay of the local arts crowd. However, since its opening it has managed to attract a steady stream of local and international productions, as well as a growing audience. It has now become one of Valletta's busiest cultural ven-

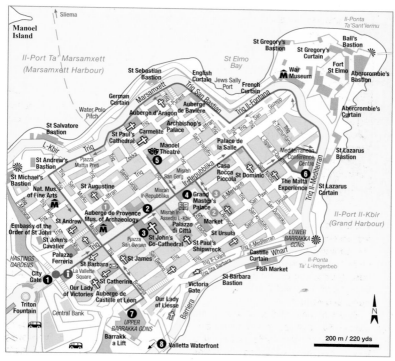

The plain facade of St John's hides a wealth of treasures inside

ues and productions are held here most weekends, especially during the summer months, when it is lovely to sit and listen to a concert or watch a dance production under the stars.

REPUBLIC STREET

As you continue straight ahead you will find yourself on the main thoroughfare, **Republic Street ②**. This is the capital's busiest street, with hundreds of shops, cafés and restaurants to keep you busy.

The first major attraction on this road is the imposing **National Museum of Archaeology** (daily 9am–6pm). It contains collections of prehistoric pottery, sculpture and personal ornaments recovered from the megalithic temples that dot the island, including Malta's famous 'Fat Ladies' – statues of overweight women that have been discovered in the island's temples and are thought to be a symbol of fertility. There are also some typical examples of tomb furniture of the Punic and Roman periods. A visit here is the perfect preamble ahead of your Temple Tour (see page 46).

If you are in need of a coffee break, head to St John's Street where you'll find **Dolce Peccati ①**, one of the city's best cafés.

St John's Co-Cathedral

Continue on to Valletta's pride and joy – the magnificent **St John's Co-Cathedral ③** (Mon–Fri 9am–4pm, Sat 9.30am–12.30pm). Designed by Maltese architect Girolamo Cassar, the cathedral was consecrated on 20 February 1578; until 1798 it was the order's conventual church. Pope Pius VII gave it the title co-cathedral in 1816 to resolve the rivalry between Mdina and Valletta, which dated back to the Knights' arrival in 1530.

Do not be fooled by its somewhat bleak facade, the interior is awe-inspiring in its wealth and detail. As you leave the sunlit square and walk through the main portal into the semi-darkness of the cathedral, the sense of contrast is striking. The rigid, plain lines of the exterior change, as if by magic, into a dazzling blaze of colour and decoration, which made Sir Walter Scott exclaim with delight in 1831: 'This is the most magnificent place I saw in my life.'

The richly painted vault, arabesque carvings covering every inch of the walls, and multi-coloured marble slabs stretching from one end of the floor to the other, may initially be overwhelming, but a sense of harmony does prevail.

Rectangular in shape, the church features a barrelled interior with chapels on either side of the central chamber. The buttressing, which Cassar hid with his exterior walls, separates the main body of the church from the side altars. The interior is best seen when empty, when the full sweep of some 400 floor sepulchre slabs can be appreciated.

The bronze lecterns, dated 1557, came from the Knights' chapter church

The frescoed ceiling of the cathedral

in Vittoriosa. The high altar, finished in 1686, is encrusted with lapis lazuli and in its centre is a bronze bas-relief of the *Last Supper*. Giuseppe Mazzuoli created the large marble group, the *Baptism of Christ*, at the end of the chancel. Seven of the eight original members of the order have their own chapel dedicated to the patron saint of the Langue and containing the tombs of the grand masters. The missing member is England; as a result of Henry VIII's fight with Rome the English Knights were withdrawn from the order.

The cathedral ceiling was bare until Mattia Preti was commissioned in 1661 to decorate it. The greatest treasure in the oratory leading to the **Church Museum** (entrance fee included in the main ticket) is a painting by Caravaggio, *The Beheading of St John the Baptist*; it is his only known signed work. The museum houses a fine collection of Flemish tapestries, silver objects and sacred vestments.

REPUBLIC SQUARE

The little stretch of road between St John's Co-Cathedral and Republic Square is home to the island's Law Courts, as well as one of Valletta's busiest malls, Embassy, down on St Lucy's Street. Embassy is also the place to go to see *Valletta Living History*, a fantastic short film on the capital's convoluted past that is entertaining for all ages.

Girolamo Cassar

The greatest Maltese architect was Girolamo Cassar (c.1520–92), whose influence and legacy was to Valletta what Christopher Wren's was to London. He designed the Grand Master's Palace, the Co-Cathedral of St John, the *auberges* of the Knights, the Hospital of the Order, the slaves' prison, the Ferreria (arsenal) and several more churches and monastic buildings; many survive today.

Before embarking on his works, Cassar was sent on a short tour of the foremost cities of Italy, and so his buildings rose in a somewhat rigid variant of Italian Mannerism. But his designs, as it transpired, also perpetuated many traditional features that appeared on early buildings in Mdina and Birgu. They set the character of all the buildings in Valletta and influenced all subsequent Maltese building and architectural enterprise.

Cassar's emphasis was strongly horizontal, with huge masses of plain masonry predominating, the whole tied in with 'rusticated' corners – that is, with sunken joints and roughened surfaces. These corners became his hallmark. Cassar also believed that all his buildings should echo the fact that they were constructed in a fortified city and have, therefore, a military cast. Even his masterpiece, the (now riotously decorated) Co-Cathedral of St John, was designed to be as severe on the inside as it is on the outside.

The impressive collection of the Palace Armoury

Just behind Republic Square is the **National Library** (Mon–Sat 8.15am–1.15pm), also known as the Biblioteca. Built in the 1790s, it was the last building erected by the Knights, and today houses important historical documents, including the charter granting the Maltese islands to the Order by Charles V of Spain in 1530. Note that you will be asked to show some form of identification – such as a passport – before being allowed in.

Outside the library stands a statue of Queen Victoria (recalling the square's former name of Queen's Square), which is surrounded by the tables of three lovely outdoor cafés. The most famous of these is **Caffè Cordina**, established in 1837, which has a fine reputation for the quality of its food and coffee – do try its wonderful home-made ice cream.

A small detour of a block back up Republic Street towards the city gate takes you to **Great Siege Square**. The large statue here is dedicated to the defenders of Malta who died during the Great Siege.

GRAND MASTER'S PALACE

The **Grand Master's Palace** ❹ sits adjacent to the Library. Just like the Co-Cathedral, if the main facade of the edifice is plain and a little disappointing, the palace's sumptuous interior more than makes up for it.

The building's exterior is covered with plaques commemorating local histor-

ical events, including the citation King George VI wrote when he awarded the island the George Cross in 1942, and a letter from the American President Franklin Roosevelt commending the islanders for their valour. The Grand Masters used the palace as their headquarters until they left the island in 1798. During the British colonial period it was the governor's headquarters. Since 1974 it has served as the office of the president and the base for parliament until it moved to its new home near City Gate.

The Palace is open to visitors, as are the **State Rooms** (Mon–Wed, Fri 10am–4pm, Sat–Sun 9am–5pm). Guards will likely show you through the arched entrance into **Neptune's Court**, with its subtropical plants. **Prince Alfred's Court**, named in honour of a visit by Queen Victoria's second son in 1858, is through an archway to the right. The clock dates from 1745; the hours are struck by figures representing Moorish slaves.

Palace highlights

To reach the public entrance to the **State Apartments** take the small steps in a corner of the courtyard. Unfortunately visitors are not allowed to use the massive stone steps once trodden by the Knights but, once on the first floor, you can see them through the glass doors to the left. The Knights used the **Tapestry Room** (first left) as their council chamber, and

The Throne Room inside the Grand Master's Palace

this is where the Maltese parliament – meeting between 1921 and 1976 – established the republican government. The tapestries in the first chamber to the left were given to the order by Grand Master Perellos in the 18th century. The friezes above the tapestries depict the Knights' galleys in battle against the Turks.

The **Throne Room**, formerly called the Hall of St Michael and St George, contains the Great Siege frescoes. Painted between 1576 and 1581, they portray the battles from the Turks' arrival at Marsaxlokk Bay until their eventual withdrawal. The small balcony on the wall opposite the throne was made from the stern of the *Grand Carrick of Rhodes*, Grand Master Adam's flagship.

The **Armoury** (daily 9am–4.30pm) is on the ground floor at the rear, near Neptune's Court. It contains one of the finest collections of weaponry in Europe, including a gold Damascene suit of armour fashioned for Grand Master Aloph de Wignacourt. Detailed audio guides are available.

You'll exit the Armoury on Merchant's Street, which has all sorts of options for lunch. Among the best are **Soul Food** ❷ and **Ambrosia** ❸.

THE PEOPLE'S THEATRE

From Republic Street turn into Old Theatre Street to find the city's iconic **Manoel Theatre** ❺ (Mon–Fri tours 10am–noon). Financed by Grand Master Manoel de Vilhena 'for the honest recreation of the people', it opened in 1732. Beautifully restored in 1969, it is believed to be the second oldest theatre in use in Europe. Now considered the island's 'national theatre' it stages

---

Valletta by night

Plan an evening in the capital and you won't be disappointed. Just 10 years ago, locals would complain about Valletta being 'dead' in the evenings; deathly quiet and uninspiring once all the city workers had gone home and the shops had closed for the evening. Today, though, it is the beloved haunt of the cultural crowd, who have made it their dynamic home. After sundown, a myriad of restaurants, wine bars, exhibition spaces and theatres open up to provide entertainment. They concentrate around Strait Street – once the Mediterranean's most notorious red-light districts. Here tens of bars and restaurants have opened in recent years, attracting a post-theatre crowd for late-night dinners and live music performances. Book ahead to secure your table at Trabuxu Wine Bar where you can enjoy a platter of cured meats, local cheese and fresh bread, then move on to City Lounge for a cocktail on the terrace overlooking St George's Square. The city is also beautifully lit at night, perfect for a romantic evening stroll.

The Upper Barrakka Gardens

plays in both English and Maltese, as well as concerts, ballets and operas. It is best to check the website (www.teatrumanoel.com.mt) for updates on the latest shows.

Back on Republic Street, **Casa Rocca Piccola** (Mon–Sat 10am–5pm) at No. 74 is one of the only patrician houses in Valletta open to the public. The house was restored by the present marquis and boasts some of the oldest examples of Maltese furniture. In the library is a set of 17th-century canvases said to have adorned the Grand Master's barge of Lascaris. In the Blue Sitting Room you can see surgical instruments used in the Knights' Hospital. We recommend the lively guided tour behind the scenes, which lasts an hour, and most Fridays 'Champagne Tours' are led by the Marquis Nicholas de Piro himself, which really adds to the experience (advance booking required).

THE MALTA EXPERIENCE AND FORT ST ELMO

From Republic Street, turn right into Triq San Nikola then up Triq Il-Merkanti and right on Triq L-Ispar Il-Qadim until you reach the ring road Triq Il-Mediterranean. The walk here shows a different side to the city's character as it is more residential, with hundreds of townhouses sitting side by side – some of which have been beautifully restored, making the most of the growing demand for real estate here.

On Triq Il-Mediterranean you'll find the Mediterranean Conference Centre, which was the 'Sacra Infermeria' or Holy Infirmary of the Knights. Built in the latter part of the 16th century, it is now used as a theatre and conference centre.

The **Malta Experience** ❻ (Mon–Fri 11am–4pm, Sat–Sun 11am–2pm) is located just across the road. This 45-minute dramatic audiovisual show, available in 15 languages, encapsulates the main events in the islands' history using the latest projection techniques.

At the tip of the peninsula, **Fort St Elmo**, erected in 1488, played a pivotal role in the defence of the islands during the first Great Siege. Although it isn't yet open to the public following its extensive restoration, occasional open days are held. Part of the fort is devoted to the **National War Museum** (daily 9am–6pm), which documents the island's resistance during World War II. Its most treasured exhibit is the actual George Cross medal conferred in 1942. This was awarded by King George VI in recognition of the 'heroism and devotion' of Malta's people during the siege. The cross is woven into the design of Malta's flag.

Another 10 minutes' walk along the ring road takes you to the **Fortifications Interpretation Centre** (summer Mon–Fri 9am–1pm, Tue and Thu till 4pm, Winter Mon–Fri 10am–4pm, Tue and Thu till 7pm, Sat 9.30–1pm). The

The Auberge de Castille

A performance at the Manoel Theatre

museum narrates the history of the bastions and fortifications that are so prevalent in Malta, and is a good rainy-day option for families too.

GARDENS WITH A VIEW

From the Fortifications Interpretation Centre, head back up to Republic Street and take a right at Pjazza Teatru Rjal. This will bring you to **De Valette Square** on your left, where stands a statue dedicated to Valletta's founder – Grand Master La Valette – as well as the first church to be built in Valletta, **Our Lady of Victories**. Beyond is Castille Square. Opposite them, **Auberge de Castille** houses the office of the Prime Minister and is not open to the public.

A short walk will lead you to the **Upper Barrakka Gardens** ❼ (daily 7am–10pm), where you can stop for a cold drink overlooking the Grand Harbour and Three Cities. This is also where you can hop onto the **Barrakka Lift** (daily June–Oct 7am–midnight, Nov–May 7am–9pm). The lift is 58 metres (190ft) high and will take you on the 25-second journey down to the **Valletta Waterfront** ❽, lined with a number of shops, bars and restaurants.

Back in Castille Place, **St James' Bastion** leads past the Central Bank of Malta to the **St James Cavalier Arts Centre**, a vibrant space that regularly hosts plays, exhibitions and concerts.

Just beyond, you'll be back to City Gate, where this route ends.

Food and drink

❶ DOLCE PECCATI

55, Triq San Gwann; tel: 2122 2012; Mon–Fri 7am–7pm, Sat–Sun 8am–3pm; €€
This Italian-run café is a favourite with locals, especially businessmen and lawyers stopping in for their morning caffeine hit, and sometimes one of the delicious Italian sweet treats – such as their trademark *casatella Siciliana* (ricotta and marzipan cake).

❷ SOUL FOOD

76, Merchants Street; tel 2123 4311; Sun–Fri 11am–6.30pm; €€

Also run by Italians, Soul Food is a good-value lunch option whose healthy menu will delight vegans and vegetarians. The pasta is arguably the best in the capital.

❸ AMBROSIA

137 Archbishop Street; tel: 2122 5923; www.vallettarestaurant.com; Mon–Sat 12.30–2.30pm and 7.30–9.30pm; €€€€
This true staple in the capital is ideal for those in search of authentic food. Run by chef patron Chris Farrugia, you'll be hard-pressed to find a menu of fresher ingredients presented in a more innovative way: fantastic Mediterranean fare, with a Maltese twist.

Along Sliema's Promenade

SLIEMA AND ST JULIAN'S

This is the most modern part of the island. Sliema is Malta's commercial centre, with its malls and shopping centres. St Julian's on the other hand is the nightlife capital. The promenade that connects them makes for a lovely walk.

DISTANCE: 4km (2.4 miles)
TIME: Half day, afternoon and evening
START: Sliema
END: St Julian's
POINTS TO NOTE: Instead of taking the bus to Sliema, you could hop onto the Valletta-to-Sliema ferry (www.vallettaferryservices.com), which runs daily every half an hour or so. The walk along the Promenade will take a good 45 minutes, so it's important to wear comfortable shoes.

Unlike most of the more popular parts of Malta, Sliema and St Julian's aren't known for their history or culture, but for their modern facilities. This should be your first port of call if you want to shop, or need any particular provisions for your stay.

SLIEMA

Today it is hard to imagine that **Sliema** ❶ used to be a quiet seaside village – in fact, its name *sliem*, derives from the Maltese word for 'peace'. Today, 'peace' doesn't exactly come to mind when you think of Sliema. It is busy and cosmopolitan, with high-rise apartment blocks, high street and designer shops, and

Festas

If you're visiting during the summer months, then it's well worth attending a local *festa* – a lovely feast paying homage to each village's patron saint. For one week each year, each village will come along with street decorations, fireworks and band marches. The parish church is always the centre of the occasion, and it is gloriously decorated inside and out with bright lights, flowers, damask curtains and chandeliers. While the dates for each feast vary slightly from year to year, the St Julian's feast – one of the most popular in this part of the island – is always held at the end of August. Visit www.maltadiocese.org for an updated list of this year's *festa* dates.

Fireworks at a fiesta in St Julian's

top restaurants. That said, if you do want to get a feel for its history, you should head inwards to the more residential streets, where you can still see some of the grand houses built here by the British and wealthy Maltese. Sliema started to gain ground as a tourist destination in the 1960s, and in the 1980s many of its beautiful old houses were torn down and replaced by flats.

The commercial part of town is set around its two main shopping streets – **Tower Road** and **Bisazza Street**, but now extends to include **The Point**, the island's largest shopping mall. Here you'll find everything from fashion shops, to homeware as well as a large indoor playing area for children.

Café culture is rife in Sliema and many come here to 'see and be seen'. This is the place for breakfast or brunch. Of the myriad establishments to choose from, a great option is the iconic **Giorgio's ❶**.

THE PROMENADE

Leaving Tower Road behind you, you'll walk up the hill past numerous other shops and onto the **Promenade ❷**. On your left your little ones will no doubt spot the children's playing area – one of the largest on the island. This is a good stop for families keen to let their little ones run around.

Alternatively, walk along the Promenade as it winds its way along the seafront, past shops, cafés and ice-cream parlours. The rocky beaches below may well entice you to have a quick dip. The most popular beach here is Exiles, which

Map labels:
- St. George's Tower
- 1000 m / 1100 yds
- Il Ponta tad-Dragunara (Dragonara Point)
- Casino
- Paceville
- Il-Qaliet
- Spinola Fort
- St. Julian's Point
- St. Julian's Tower
- St. Julian's ❸
- Spinola Bay
- Balluta Bay
- SLIEMA ❶
- Sliema Point Tower
- Stella Maris
- Sacred Heart
- Promenade ❷
- Gzira
- Sliema Creek
- Manoel Island
- Tigne Fort
- University
- Fort Manoel
- Marsamxett Harbour
- Ta' Xbiex
- Lazaretto Creek
- VALLETTA

Boats in Spinola Bay

lies at the foot of **St Julian's Tower**, yet another watchtower built by the Knights.

If you're hungry stop at **U Bistrot** ②, a roadside café and restaurant half-way between Sliema and St Julian's serving fresh and healthy fare.

ST JULIAN'S

Entering **St Julian's** ❸ you'll find yourself in pretty **Spinola Bay**, with its iconic 'LOVE statue' on the prom-enade. Just like Sliema, St Julian's has changed a lot in recent years – morphing from a fishing village into a buzzing town. Spinola Bay is where you'll find many of the best restau-rants, including **Gululu** ❸, which is renowned for its authentic Maltese cuisine.

Further up the hill you'll see the Portomaso Tower, the tallest building in Malta, and beyond that Paceville – the island's nightlife capital. Popular with the teen and twenty-something crowd, there are streets of clubs and bars that stay open long into the early morning.

Follow the road down St Rita's Steps to Baystreet, another popu-lar mall which houses various chain stores including Aldo, Guess and Accessorize, as well as numerous din-ing options. The mall sits right by **St George's Bay** – the only sandy beach in the area and with a Blue Flag sta-tus to boot.

Food and drink

❶ GIORGIO'S

Tigné Seafront, Sliema; tel: 2134 2456; daily 7am–midnight; €€
The archetypal Sliema café, this corner spot has attracted patrons for decades, and remains very popular. The coffee is served piping hot to accompany your choice of snack or Mediterranean fare.

❷ U BISTROT

George Borg Olivier Street, Sliema; tel 2311 2361; www.facebook.com/UBistrot; Mon–Fri 10am–11pm, Sat–Sun 9am–midnight; €€€

The team here is dedicated to producing and cooking real food, and their specials change daily. The focus is on food that's fresh, succulent and full of texture. Their salads are some of the best on the island.

❸ GULULU

133, Spinola Bay; tel: 2133 3431; www.gululu.com.mt; daily 6–11pm, Sat–Sun noon–5pm also; €€€
Right on the seafront and wholly dedicated to traditional Maltese cooking, Gululu is a must if you want a taste of genuine local fare. The pizzas and bread dishes are all baked in a traditional Maltese baker's stone oven.

Fort St Angelo, Vittoriosa

THE THREE CITIES

Once home to the Knights, and later to the great dockyards that kept the British Mediterranean Navy afloat, today the Three Cities remain one of Malta's most atmospheric areas, with a pleasing mix of old and new.

DISTANCE: 5km (3.1 miles)
TIME: Full day
START: Senglea
END: Kalkara
POINTS TO NOTE: Although transport around the Three Cities has improved, it will still help to have a car as you explore the areas further afield. As an alternative to taking the bus, you could hop abroad the Valletta–Three Cities ferry (daily; www.vallettaferryservices.com), which will certainly ensure you avoid the rush hour traffic.

No trip to Malta is complete without some time spent in The Three Cities. This is one of the few places that – in many ways – still feels untouched; yet it is also a chic destination for fantastic food and wine – arguably the perfect combination.

The Three Cities were originally called il-Birgu, l-Isla and Bormla. They were renamed Vittoriosa, Senglea and Cospicua respectively after the Great Siege, and the names are pretty much interchangeable today. The fortifications that surround Cospicua are the result of several centuries of building in the wake of the siege. The Margherita Lines which ran from French Creek to Kalkara Creek were designed by Marculano da Firenzuola in 1638; the outer Cotonera Lines, which form a semi-circle with a circumference of 5km (3 miles), were built between 1670 and 1680. The two rings formed a secure line of defence in which over 40,000 people could be housed in times of war. Today most of the bastions are surrounded by apartment buildings and have had tunnels dug through them for traffic access.

SENGLEA

This route starts in Senglea. From Sliema and Valletta, drivers should follow signs to the airport and Three Cities; at the Three Cities roundabout take the Paola exit (the first one). Stay on this road until the second roundabout, then take the Cospicua exit,

drive through St Helen's Gate in the Margherita Bastions, and park on St Paul Square. To get into **Senglea ❶**, walk along Triq Il-Mons. Claude de la Sengle, after whom the city is named, fortified the city in 1554 and also built Fort St Michael.

After Fort St Elmo fell during the Great Siege, both Fort St Michael (dismantled in 1922) and Fort St Angelo became the primary targets of Ottoman guns, and a great chain was stretched across the points of the 'fingers' with a bridge of boats that allowed the defenders to move men easily between the two. The peninsula was bombarded again during World War II when the nearby dry docks were a target.

Inside the gates, on the left, is **Our Lady of Victory Church**. The modern monument is dedicated to the Three Cities residents killed in 1940–43. Just beyond, take a left up the steps of **Triq San Pietru u San Pawl** and peer over the wall at the end for a direct look into the heart of the docks.

Return to the main street; on **Pjazza L-Er-bgha Ta' Settembru**

is a copy of the Madonna and Child statue which used to stand in front of Our Lady of Victory Church. This is often called the 'Miracle Madonna' because it remained unscathed by bombs. Stop for a moment and look at the pleasing pattern the balconies make as they lead the eye up Triq il-Vittorja toward the Baroque **St Philip's Church** on Pjazza Francesco Zahra Pittur.

Turn right at the church then left on Triq Iz-Zewg Mini and you will

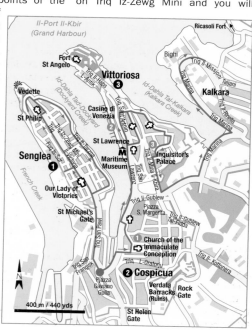

Looking across to Valletta from the Vedette lookout

soon arrive at the **Safe Haven Garden**, with its wonderful views over the harbour to Valletta. At the tip of the promontory stands the **Vedette**, the famous old sentry post. Carved on to the vedette are an oversized eye and ear, symbols of vigilance, as well as a pelican, a symbol for Christian love. At the park entrance, descend the steps to the left for a walk round the point.

Along this pleasant walkway, you will stumble across boating clubs where members work on their *dghajjes* – the distinctive boats reminiscent of Venetian gondolas and highly decorated in bright colours. Today they feature in annual boat races but there was a time when these boats worked as ferries, transporting people between the towns that surround the Grand Harbour.

Retrace your steps around the tip. Towards the head of the bay, stepped streets lead steeply upwards. The archway ahead signals the end of Senglea.

COSPICUA

Thanks to the **Dock One** project, an €11 million rehabilitation of this area, you can now walk all the way around this bay to reach **Cospicua ❷**. **Nuovo Café San Giorgio ❶**, overlooking a lovely piazza, is a good place for a quick snack if you're feeling peckish.

Cospicua took the brunt of the bombardment in World War II: over 90 percent of the town was flattened.

While many of the buildings still look dilapidated, others are being done up and transformed, which has helped the area, and the whole of the Three Cities, to become a real estate hot spot in recent years.

The Dock One project has given Cospicua a new lease of life; you can enjoy a walk along the promenade, with its new lawn, laced with benches should you want to sit and relax here for a while.

VITTORIOSA

At the crest of the hill is **Vittoriosa ❸**, known in medieval times as Birgu and the first Sicilian–Norman capital. When the Knights arrived in 1530, they made Birgu their base. After the Great Siege, the city was renamed Vittoriosa, but when the Knights moved to their new capital, Valletta, the power structure went with them.

At the end of the street into Vittoriosa, palm trees surround the four statues of the Freedom Monument, which commemorates the withdrawal of the British forces in 1979. Before exploring the church behind it, head to the splendid colonnaded building that once housed the old navy bakery. It is now the **Maritime Museum** (daily 9am–5pm), which features collections of model ships, actual Maltese boats and many exhibits dealing with the maritime history of the Maltese Islands, from the Phoenicians to the British occupation. The **Vittoriosa**

Vittoriosa harbour and the Church of St Lawrence

Waterfront has become a true highlight of this area. The numerous restaurants and cafés along here are popular with the yachting community as well as with locals. The marina has been transformed and now welcomes every type of boat from dinky dinghies to massive super yachts, many of which have made Malta their base. **La Marina** ❷, on the waterfront, is a good spot for lunch.

Leaving the Maritime Museum, walk towards **Fort St Angelo**, which houses a museum detailing the forts history and offers wonderful views over the Grand Harbour.

Back in the square fronting the church, **St Lawrence** was the first conventual church of the Order and it contains many relics of the Knights. Built in 1723 to replace a smaller church erected by Count Roger the Norman, it is a magnificent building in a picturesque corner.

The steps to the left of the church lead to St Joseph and then into **Victory Square**. The Knights' Auberge d'Allemagne is situated on the corner of the square at Triq Hilda Tabone (also called Britannic); next to it is the Auberge d'Angleterre; across the street is the Auberge d'Auvergne et de Provence and, several buildings up, the Auberge de France with its portal by Bartolomeo Genga.

The Inquisitor's Palace

Return to Victory Square and head to Triq Il-Palazz Ta' l-Isqof, where you will find the entrance to the **Inquisitor's Palace** (daily 9am–5pm) on the right.

The Inquisition or Holy Office was established in Malta in 1562. As the Pope's delegate, the Inquisitor was accommodated in style. Though its role was to combat heresy and protect the Catholic faith, this office was not as dogmatic when it was first established as the infamous Spanish Inquisition. It was only as the Inquisitor's power base grew stronger than it took on a more ruthless role. Of the island's 62 inquisitors, two became popes, and 22 attained the cardinal's red hat. The inquisitors beat a hasty retreat when the French conquered the island in 1798. In the 19th century the building was used as officers' quarters. The present building was constructed in the 1530s and, today, houses a fascinating exhibition of items related to historic law. It also houses permanent Good Friday and Christmas exhibitions, featuring traditional items that were used to celebrate these special periods in the Maltese religious calendar.

Nearby, **Tal-Petut Restaurant** ❸ is a great place to enjoy Vittoriosa by night over a glass of wine.

KALKARA

You have two options here: to leave Vittoriosa via the **Gate of Provence** and return to your car (or wait for a bus at the nearby stop), or turn left

Quiet Vittoriosa backstreet

and continue down the hill. The latter means leaving the Three Cities, but tiny **Kalkara** is definitely worth seeing.

Many of Malta's traditional boats are repaired here or are wintered alongside the few craftsmen who still build the traditional *dghajsa* once used to ferry passengers to and from ships berthed in Grand Harbour.

The large church that sits at the head of Kalkara Creek is the beautifully austere St Joseph. The main sanctuary is made of local sandstone. The altar is bare except for a set of candlesticks and a statue of Christ.

Climb the hill towards the graceful 19th-century neoclassical **Bighi Hospital**, where the wounded troops of Napoleon and Nelson were treated.

During World War I the hospital was known as the 'Nurse of the Mediterranean'. In the Great Siege a Turkish battery operated from **Fort Ricasoli**, on the seaward point across Rinella Creek.

The **Malta Film Studios** located here have helped give Malta its name as the 'Hollywood of the Mediterranean', as many high-profile blockbusters have been filmed here, and on the island, in recent years, including series one of *Game of Thrones* and *Murder on the Orient Express*. Film-makers can make use of the studios' two large water tanks, both overlooking the sea. One is a specifically designed deep-water photography tank where scenes can be shot underwater in controlled conditions.

Food and drink

❶ NUOVO CAFÉ SAN GIORGIO
Bormla Promenade; tel: 9911 0113; Tue–Sun 9.30am–10pm; €€
This Italian restaurant and café boasts an unbeatable location. From breakfast to dinner it buzzes with locals. Situated in a little square, their outdoor terrace is a beautiful place to spend a summer evening.

❷ LA MARINA
Vittoriosa Waterfront; tel: 2180 9909; daily 10am–11pm; €€€

The good Italian food here is made even better by the restaurant's glorious setting overlooking the marina. The menu is predominantly fish based, and there is a good wine list to accompany it.

❸ TAL-PETUT RESTAURANT
20 P.Scicluna, tel: 2189 1169; www.talpetut.com; Mon–Sat 6.30–10pm; €€
Tal-Petut specialises in freshly-cooked local dishes with a strong Mediterranean influence. You will find a friendly and welcoming wait staff in a comfortable, romantic and cosy setting.

The Tarxien Temples

THE TEMPLE REGION

*Malta's prehistoric temples are believed to be some of the oldest stone structures
in the world and have thus been jointly declared a Unesco World Heritage Site.
Combine this with the ancient Hypogeum burial ground and a boat ride through
the Blue Grotto, and you're in for a perfect day.*

DISTANCE: 9km (5.5 miles)
TIME: Half or full day
START: Hypogeum
END: Blue Lagoon
POINTS TO NOTE: While there are
buses to this region, a car is really
essential if you want to be able to get
around at your own pace, so it's best to
hire one or to book a chauffeured taxi.

Malta isn't called a 'living museum' for
nothing. Its prehistoric treasures date
back thousands of years, harking to
a time we know very little about. That
said, a visit to these ancient temples
and burial grounds can help to shed a
little light on the processes that were
used back then and the beliefs that surrounded them.

THE HYPOGEUM

Start your journey in Tarxien, the location
of the Hypogeum. A Unesco World Heritage Site in its own right (distinct from the
rest of the Unesco-listed temples) this

is one of the most impressive historic
treasures that Malta has to offer, so it's
surprising, and regrettable, how many
people don't make the trip to see it.

The **Hal Saflieni Hypogeum** ❶ (daily
9am–5pm) is an underground burial
complex that was first used in 3600BC.
Historians believe that more than
7,000 people were buried here over
a number of centuries. Today you'll be
able to wander from chamber to chamber across three levels, listening to the
audio-guide as you go along. The lowest level is 10.6 meters (34.7ft) below
ground and temperature-controlled.
Tickets to the Hypogeum are limited and
you must book ahead, ideally online at
www.heritagemalta.org. Children under
five are not admitted.

Just a few hundred metres away
are the **Tarxien Temples** (daily
9am–5pm). This group of four temples
is remarkable for the quality of its carvings, which include not only subtle dec-
orative spirals, but also friezes of farm
animals – among them a bull, crafted
to represent virility, and a suckling sow,
representing fertility.

Carvings at Tarxien   *Hagar Qim, the Standing Stones*

Before heading off, pop into the nearby **Traffic Lights Café ❶** for a bite to eat.

MNAJDRA

The next stop on this temple tour is Qrendi. A left turn a few hundred metres/ yards up from the entrance of the town leads to **Hagar Qim ❷**, also known as the 'Standing Stones'. This prehistoric temple overlooking the sea was constructed with globigerina limestone, and some of the slabs are among the largest in the world. The complex is almost completely surrounded by a curtain wall, with three massive standing stones set into it. The Maltese Venus, the statue of the Seated Woman and several other female figurines were found here. They now reside in the Archaeological Museum in Valletta (see page 32). As a temple of the Ggantija period, Hajar Qim actually pre-dates Stonehenge in England and the Pyramids in Egypt. It also features carvings that do not appear anywhere else in Malta.

Neighbouring **Mnajdra ❸**, the sister temple, also enjoys a beautiful site overlooking the sea. Look out for Filfla, opposite, the uninhabited island nature reserve that was once used by the British army as a firing range. Dating from 3000BC–1500BC, Mnajdra was built from coralline limestone and consists of three temples, with a common outside wall. Seen from above, the chambers of the middle temple resemble a woman's body. People believed that a fertility goddess's control of the elements ensured a fruitful harvest. The temples were used for sacrificial purposes, and gifts of milk and blood were presented at the altars. Note the square holes in the Oracle chamber, behind which hidden priests spoke to worshippers. This is a good place for a picnic and, in the early evening, for watching the sunset.

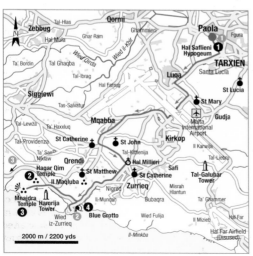

Boat trip to the Blue Grotto

THE BLUE GROTTO

Leave Mnajdra and head to Zurrieq and on to the charming **Blue Grotto** ❹, which is less than a five minutes' drive away. Consisting of several caves and grottoes, the best time to go is in the early morning, when the light reflected through the caves brings out the colour.

From the car park follow signs to the mooring dock. This is where you'll be able to hitch a ride on a little boat and head out to sea to enjoy the superb vistas and get a closer view of Filfla. The tiny boats run daily between 9am and 4.30pm, weather permitting, and each journey takes around 25 minutes. Bear in mind that these boat trips are in high demand during the summer months, so you may have to wait in line.

After your boat trip, head to the tiny rocky inlet of **Wied iz-Zurrieq**. Here, traditional Maltese *luzzu* fishing boats are moored in the water or hauled ashore to be repainted in fine colours. You'll also find a number of restaurants, bars and souvenir handicraft shops. The clear waters that lie between the Wied and the small island of Filfla provide excellent diving conditions.

If it's time for lunch, the **Blue Cave Restaurant** ❷ at the top of the hill makes great pizzas, while **Carmen`s Bar and Restaurant** ❸ is ideal if you fancy something a little more upmarket.

Food and drink

❶ TRAFFIC LIGHTS CAFÉ

Paola Square, Paola; tel: 2713 3642; www.trafficlightscafe.com; Mon–Fri 7am–7pm, Sat 7am–3pm; €€

This little café may not be much from the outside but it is a great place for brunch or a quick snack. The coffee is good quality and so are the cakes. There are heartier options too, including pasta, if you fancy something more substantial.

❷ BLUE CAVE RESTAURANT

Wied iz-Zurrieq; tel 2164 7909; Thu–Tue 9am–midnight, Wed 9am–6pm; €€

Right by the Blue Grotto, it is a convenient place for a quick bite to eat after your boat tour. Friendly and laidback, this establishment is known for its pizzas, grilled meats, fresh fish and great seafood.

❸ CARMEN`S BAR AND RESTAURANT

4 Ghar Lapsi, Siggiewi; tel: 9940 4121; Mon, Wed–Sat 11.30am–11pm, Sun 11.30am–7pm; €€€

Combining some outstanding views with top-quality Mediterranean cuisine, this is a dining experience you will cherish. The chefs always make the most of the freshest local ingredients, while the setting, overlooking the cliffs and sea, is truly superb. Perfect for a special occasion.

Busy Birzebbuga

THE SOUTH

Spend your day exploring the fishing villages of the south, where you can swim in some of the clearest waters and enjoy a delicious fish lunch.

DISTANCE: 9km (5.5 miles)
TIME: Full day
START: Birzebbugia
END: Marsaskala
POINTS TO NOTE: Public transport to the south of Malta is frequent and, most of the time, reliable; yet some landmarks and bays mentioned below are easier to get to by car or taxi. It is also recommended that you carry a map with you at all times, in case you get lost. A good pair of shoes and loads of sun cream are essential.

The south of Malta is considered to be among the island's most unspoilt destinations, and isn't usually part of the typical tourist trail. A visit here will give you the opportunity to see the natural side of the island, to explore the countryside and to try the more local swimming haunts, instead of the touristy ones. Because there aren't any major hotels in the area, you'll be able to mingle with locals and get a real taster for life in Malta.

BIRZEBBUGA

Start your day in **Birzebbuga** ❶, the island's southernmost village. This is a lovely village but its charm is almost overwhelmed by the presence of the giant freeport container terminal. This is one of Malta's most important sources of income after tourism and here the two clash in spectacular visual juxtaposition. Thankfully, this hasn't made it any less popular with locals or visitors. Look out for the marker near Kalafrana, which commemorates the summit between Mikhail Gorbachev and George Bush Snr that marked the end of the Cold War between the US and the Soviet Union on 23 December 1989 (just a few weeks after the fall of the Berlin Wall). This was held on the SS *Maxim Gorkiy* cruiser moored in Marsaxlokk Bay.

Just beyond, Pretty Bay is a white sandy beach ringed with attractively painted homes – it is the ideal spot for some morning sunbathing. If you're hungry, pop into the popular **Bite Size Café** ❶ where you can enjoy breakfast

Marsaxlokk's Sunday market

with a view of the lovely beach and the container terminal.

For a more cultural pursuit, head up the hill towards **Borg in-Nadur** ❷ (open by appointment; tel: 2295 4000), a site of such archaeological importance that an entire prehistoric phase was named after it. This temple was built during the last phase of the temple period, around 2500BC, and was used by the Bronze Age people; it was likely that it then became part of a Bronze Age village. The megaliths forming the walls are now only about 50cm (1.6 feet) high and a four-apse plan can be seen at the centre. If this whets your appetite for exploring Malta's other, larger temples, then consider a day trip along the Temple Trail (see page 46).

MARSAXLOKK

Further along the coastal road brings you to the picturesque fishing village of **Marsaxlokk** ❸ (pronounced *Marsa-shlock*), set on the crest of a hill in a sheltered bay off Delimara Point. It derives its name from the word *marsa*, which means port, and the word *xlokk*, which means east, in Maltese.

The town has a long history dating back to the 9th century, when it was the first bay to welcome the Phoenicians. This was also the spot where the Turkish fleet anchored during the Great Siege. Today it holds Malta's largest fishing fleet, and the harbour, with its multitude of colourful *lazzus* (traditional fishing boats), is a photographer's dream. Walking round the bay you will see fishermen cleaning their boats, untangling nets and going about their business as they have for centuries.

Marsaxlokk is renowned for its Sunday market, which also opens during the week, with fruits and vegetables

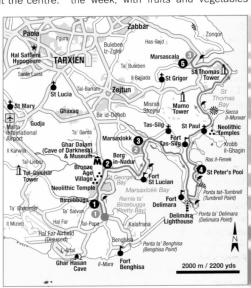

for the locals and lace for the coach parties. On Sundays, the market showcases a delightful variety of traditional Maltese produce, from handicrafts to homemade delicacies, as well as more mundane everyday items.

There is no doubt that Marsaxlokk is the best place on the island for a traditional fish lunch. **Ir-Rizzu** ❷, on the main promenade, is a favourite with the locals.

AFTERNOON BATHING

Visitors with a car should leave Marsaxlokk via the Valletta road. Those on foot should follow the bay, staying well above the power station. Just after the church take a right on Triq San Giuseppe, then another on Triq Melquart. At the roundabout at the top of the hill take the first exit and stay to the left. Some 100 metres (330ft) further take a right turn for **Delimara**, which boasts an historic fort At the first fork in the track take a right for Point Delimara (left goes to the lighthouse). Driving along the crest, you will be rewarded with wonderful views of Marsaxlokk and Birzebbuga. Note a sign pointing the way to the car park for Peter's Pool.

The road ends at Fort Delimara, not much further on. A few options here: for a more private swimming experience walk down to **Slug's Pool** or **Long Bay**; otherwise head for the more popular **St Peter's Pool** ❹.

The path down to the pool is well trodden. There's no sand, not even a shore, but if you want to swim in a glorious natural lido then this is the place to come. Just jump or dive into the deep, clear, blue water from the rocky shelving and watch where the locals get out. But stay away from the currents, which swirl under the rocky outcrops at the pool's end. If swimming is not your thing, there are some good coastal paths to explore and it's easy to find your way.

After a picnic and a swim, return to the main road and follow the signs to **St Thomas Bay**. At the next major junction (with Zejtun to the left), take a right for a meandering trip through uninhabited countryside. If on foot, take the more direct path along the shore to St Thomas Bay. Among carpets of wild flowers are saltpans, concealed bays, a communications satellite and the ruins of St Paul's Church. At St Thomas

Friendly locals

Marsascala harbour, with its tall Italianate campanile

Bay continue around the water or go directly to Marsascala.

MARSASCALA

The ancient fishing village of **Marsascala** ❺ is another example of a Maltese town blending the old with the new. Historical finds highlight the area's past, some dating back to the Roman era. In 1614, a fleet of Turkish ships made a surprise attack on the harbour – but the Maltese fought back and won.

It is worth taking a walk to see the many fortifications that were built to help defend this seaside town. The earliest watchtower, Vendôme Battery, dates to about 1715. The nearby **St Thomas Tower** is worth a visit. It was commissioned by Grand Master Alof de Wignacourt. It is a much bigger tower than the ones usually seen on the coast as it was designed to both defend the bay and store arms, and not just as a look-out tower. Zonqor Battery also lies in the area while the wonderfully preserved Briconet Redoubt, located near Marsaskala's parish church, is used as a police station.

Today, though, life in Marsascala is more about the joys of the Mediterranean than about its history. Most modern visitors prefer to amble along the promenade at dusk, enjoying the lively atmosphere. To end up this route with a drink or food platter head to **47 Summer Nights** ❸, a bar with a view favoured by locals for its laid-back atmosphere and good food.

Food and drink

❶ BITE SIZE CAFÉ

Summit Square, Birzebbuga; tel: 2165 3815; Tue–Sat 9am–midnight, Sun 9am–11pm; €
The ideal spot for breakfast with a view. Tuck into a typical local *ftira* (sandwich) with the filling of your choice or even the full English – which will really set you up for the day ahead. Equally good for lunch, dinner or a snack.

❷ IR-RIZZU

Marsaxlokk Waterfront; tel 2165 1569; daily 11.30am–3pm and Mon–Sat 6.30–11pm; €€€

This family-run fish restaurant is easily one of the best along the promenade. The generous seafood platter is the ideal starter, followed by the catch of the day – which will have been caught just a couple of hours earlier.

❸ 47 SUMMER NIGHTS

Mifsud Bonnici Square, Marsaskala; tel: 2163 9904; daily 11am–11pm; €€
Perfect for a drink, laid-back dinner or to watch the match on the big screen, this family-run restaurant and bar attracts a predominantly local crowd. The menu will prove pleasing whatever you fancy, with a good mix of pasta, fish, meat and vegetarian dishes.

The fine Palazzo Parisio gardens

THE CENTRE

The heart of Malta is made up of lots of little towns and villages, many of which can be explored on one busy day out. This route will take you to four of those villages, starting in Naxxar and finishing in the lush Presidential Gardens, taking in the historic Palazzo Parisio, the Mosta Dome, Balzan and Lija.

DISTANCE: 11km (6 miles)
TIME: Full day
START: Naxxar
END: San Anton Gardens
POINTS TO NOTE: The 43 bus will take you from Valletta to Naxxar in about 30 minutes, and you'll be able to explore on foot for most of the rest of the route. If you'd rather not splash out on food, pack a picnic to be enjoyed in San Anton Gardens. There's a kiosk just outside that sells basic refreshments too.

Despite being very close in proximity, you will probably be surprised by how distinctive each of Malta's towns and villages actually are. Naxxar and Mosta may lie side by side but both have their own distinctive attractions and traditions. Balzan, Attard and Lija, meanwhile, are collectively known as the 'Three Villages' as they blend into one another almost seamlessly. There is plenty to explore in the centre, so do make the effort to journey to this slightly more undiscovered part of the island.

NAXXAR

Dating back to prehistory, Naxxar (pronounced *Nash-shar*) is a popular town. The area is thought to have got its name from the shipwreck of St Paul, as the villagers are said to have helped St Paul and to have been among the first locals that he converted to Christianity.

Today it is a busy residential and commercial district. Start your visit at Our Lady of Victory. This parish church of prodigious size was completed in 1616 by Tomasso Dingli, a prolific boy-wonder architect who distinguished himself with several notable churches in this part of the island. The church here is home to a number of beautiful artworks, including Mattia Preti's *Birth of Our Lady*. It is worth spending an hour or two walking through the narrow – and busy – alleys around the church.

Palazzo Parisio

Opposite is the town's highlight, **Palazzo Parisio** ❶ (daily 9am–5.30pm).

The grand marble staircase inside Palazzo Parisio

Built in the 19th century by Marquis Guiseppi Scicluna, it is an outstanding example of a Maltese stately home, and the finest of its kind open to the public. It is said that its construction and furnishings set new standards for the island, and certainly its carved Lombardy furniture, stucco friezes, painted ceilings and Carrara marbles are remarkable. The great marble coping stone over the balustrade is the longest single piece on the island and had to be transported by countless mules. The palazzo's gardens are a true delight, brimming with both indigenous and exotic flowers.

Today Palazzo Parisio is still in family hands. The Scicluna family has successfully transformed it into a thriving business – between the museum and the charming **Luna Collection** tearooms and restaurant there is always a reason to visit. If you prefer something a little less fancy for lunch head to **Flora's Café** ❶ opposite.

MOSTA

A leisurely walk from Naxxar to Mosta will take around 20 minutes along 21st September Avenue – a route dotted with lots of little boutiques, shops and the odd café.

Mosta Dome

The focal point of Mosta is the **Mosta Dome** ❷ (Mon–Sat 9–11.45am, 3–5pm) – or, to give it its correct title, the Church of Santa Marija Assunta –

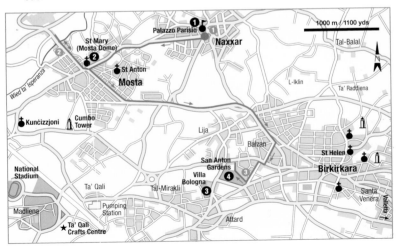

The impressive Mosta Dome

which can be seen from almost any vantage point in Malta. The islanders take great pride in its impressive scale. At 37 meters (122ft) in diameter, it is the fourth largest unsupported dome in Europe, surpassed only by Rome's Pantheon and St Peter's and the Basilica Xewkija in Gozo.

The church was completed in 1860, amid great controversy to the design of Giorgio Grognet de Vasse who chose a round church rather than a church shaped like a Latin cross. Its generous size came about because it was erected around a church already existing on the site. The original one had become too small for the growing parish but could not be demolished until an alternative was available.

As you come in, look up to admire the ceiling, which is decorated with a lovely geometric diamond pattern. Some visitors are so taken by the dome that they neglect the rest of the church, which is a shame. Do take the time to wander around.

During the heavy bombardments of World War II, a bomb pierced the dome while the church was crammed full of parishioners sheltering from the air raid. It skidded across the floor but, miraculously, did not explode. A replica is on display in the church to the left of the right altar.

While the Dome is definitely Mosta's main attraction, you could easily while away a couple of hours wandering its main streets. The town is known for its snack shops, notably **Olympic Bar** ②, on the main thoroughfare. Join locals here for a light lunch and glass of sweet tea.

THE THREE VILLAGES

It may only take around 30 minutes to walk from Mosta to Balzan, but it is recommended to take the bus, as this route is particularly traffic-heavy. The 31, 34, 41 or 42 will take you directly to the centre of Balzan in a matter of minutes.

The exquisite geometrical patterned interior of Mosta Dome

Lija's parish church

Balzan

Balzan, along with Lija and Attard, make up the 'Three Villages'. Despite the promising olde-worlde title, don't expect to see villages in the conventional sense. Indeed, you will be hard pressed even to distinguish one community from the other. In recent years the three have grown into one virtually amorphous mass, with their boundary lines known only to the residents.

As with most Maltese towns, **Balzan** was built around the parish church. This one is dedicated to the Annunciation of Our Lady and was built in the mid-17th century. Look out for the restored statue of Maria Assunta, which sits at the front of the church.

If you have children in tow, they will enjoy playing in the parish playground, just by the church. The park here is also ideal for a quick drink before you continue your walk up Main Street passing by all the grand palazzos and lovely character houses that are typical of the area.

Lija

As you reach the top of Main Street you will see a crossroads. Walk along Giuseppe Cali Street into **Lija**, which is another picturesque spot to explore. Lija is part of an urban conservation zone, which means development is very limited here. As a result, it has retained its traditional feel, and most houses have bright wooden balconies and large gardens full of citrus trees.

The parish church, dedicated to Our Saviour, looks over the Belveder, a short walk down the road. This architectural gem often nicknamed 'the wedding cake' by locals once formed part of the grand Villa Gourigion owned by Marquis Depiro.

GARDENS AND PALACES

Back up Giuseppe Cali Street and to the main crossroads, this time head towards **Attard**. The area is exclusive and home to the president's official residence. The **President's Kitchen Garden** (daily 9am–7pm) here was originally part of the President's private gardens, supplying the residence with vegetables since medieval times. Since it has opened to the public it has become very popular with families, as they enjoy a visit to its small petting zoo and playing area as well as to the lovely café.

Further along this road is **Villa Bologna** ❸ (Mon–Fri 9am–5pm, Sat 9am–1pm), one of the island's grandest stately homes. Although the house isn't actually open to the public, the gardens are, and they are absolutely beautiful. Your tour of the residence starts at the gift shop and pottery workshop, where you can pick up an iPad to guide you through the grounds. Highlights include the incredible cactus display and the recently-restored Baroque nymphaeum. The café here is also very pleasant for a cup of tea and

San Anton's Eagle Fountain   *Topiary at San Anton Gardens*

a slice of cake, although the opening times can be erratic.

Continue to **San Anton Gardens** ❹ (daily 7am–7pm) – the official gardens adjacent to the President's Palace, San Anton Palace. The palace had various roles through the decades: it served as the country residence of the Grand Masters from the early 17th century and in the British colonial era it was used as the governor's residence. Since 1974, it has been the official home of the republic's president.

The gardens showcase an astonishing assortment of subtropical flowers. Walking in an anti-clockwise direction, you'll come across the Eagle Fountain, adorned with cherubs. Straight ahead you'll see the main central pond and the palace entrance. The inviting terrace in front of the palace is backed by an ivy-covered wall. Two stone chairs flank the entrance. The only part of the palace open to the public is the colonnade leading to a back entrance of the gardens. The green doors on the right lead to the president's office. To complete your tour, pop into **Melita Gardens** ❸ for a drink or bite to eat (the pizzas are delicious).

Food and drink

❶ FLORA'S CAFÉ
1, Victory Square, Naxxar; tel: 2141 0020; Mon–Tue 8.30am–7pm, Wed–Fri 8.30am–10pm, Sat–Sun 9am–6pm; €€
Located in a traditional and restored Maltese townhouse just off the parish square, Flora's has become the 'it' place for home-made treats, cakes (especially their signature cupcakes), scones and lunches. A special weekend breakfast menu is available on Saturdays and Sundays.

❷ OLYMPIC BAR
Constitution Street, Mosta; tel 2143 2067; daily 5am–5.30pm, Sat until midnight; €
Cheap and cheerful, this is considered one of the best spots for *ftira* on the island. *Ftira* is a Maltese bread famous for its crusty exterior and soft interior. Olympic serves the freshest bread possible with a variety of fillings, including the typical mix of *kunserva* (sweet tomato paste), tuna, olives, capers and olive oil. Wash it down with some Kinnie, Malta's local soft drink.

❸ MELITA GARDENS
Idmejda Street, Balzan; tel: 2147 0663; Sun–Thu 10am–11pm, Fri–Sat 10am–10pm; €€
Combining a main restaurant, café, pizzeria and wine lounge, the food on offer is eclectic and will suit all tastes. The menu features cheesecakes and Italian cakes, as well as delicious pasta and grilled meats. The wine bar is perfect for a drink to wind down in the evening after your tour of the area.

Aerial view of Mdina, Malta's former capital

MDINA, RABAT AND DINGLI

Malta's former capital Mdina is a time capsule of medieval palazzi and world unto itself, while beneath neighbouring Rabat lie fascinating underground discoveries.

DISTANCE: 3.9km (2.4 miles)
TIME: Full day
START: Mdina
END: Dingli Cliffs
POINTS TO NOTE: While this route takes place by day, Mdina is also particularly enjoyable at night – when the dim lights create an eerie and romantic atmosphere. Whether day or night, make sure to wear comfortable shoes as most roads here are cobbled.

Many Maltese will tell you that Mdina is their favourite part of the island – and it's easy to see why. Combining historic interest and a unique personality like nowhere else in Malta, Mdina will literally transport you back in time. Mdina has enough to keep you busy for a morning, with museums and a variety of attractions. If time allows, do add Rabat and Dingli to your itinerary; they are both so completely different to the rest of the island that it would be a shame to miss them.

MDINA

Because of its commanding position on a high ridge that runs along the southwest of the island, there have been settlements here since the Bronze Age. At over 150 metres (500ft) above sea level, the area has always been easy to defend, while below, it is surrounded by fertile fields able to produce abundant vegetables and fruit to satisfy a growing population.

It is best reached by car, following the signs to Triq il-Mdina (Mdina Road); there is plenty of parking close by, in the car parks near the children's playing area or below the bastion walls. Alternatively, take the number 51 or 52 bus from Valletta to the terminus, which will stop near the city's formidable Mdina Gate.

Mdina's history sets it apart from the rest of the island. It was the site of Bronze Age settlements and, during the Roman era, Mdina and Rabat, at the time only city, was the island's capital. In the late 9th century, the Agh-

labid Arabs built the defensive ditch that bisects the city, and it was they who named the fortified part 'il Medina' (The Fortified). The Normans, who retained Mdina as their capital, later strengthened the fortifications and built magnificent churches and palaces.

The arrival of the Knights in 1530 transformed the status of Mdina. The Knights, whose power base was the small town of Birgu (today's Vittoriosa), assumed positions of leadership. With the building of Valletta, Mdina became known as Citta Vecchia (Old City). During the era of British sovereignty Mdina was no longer a centre of power, but it remained the home of Malta's noble families. Today it is a fine example of a walled medieval city. The homes have been maintained by their owners, the churches by the faithful, and Mdina remains a place of serene repose – hence its nickname, the Silent City.

The torches you see beside the doors of numerous houses are replicas of medieval streetlights. Mdina is famed for its door-knockers and the grillework that covers the windows of many a smart residence.

ENTERING THE CITY

This route starts easily enough at the **Main Gate ❶**. A Baroque triumphal archway with imposing pillars, rich carving and an ornate superstructure, it was reached by drawbridge across a dry moat. This moat was recently landscaped into a pretty garden. Inside is **St Publius Square**, named in honour of Malta's first Christian, who also became one of its patron saints (St Paul and St Agatha are the others).

MDINA, RABAT AND DINGLI **59**

To the left of the square is the **Torre dello Standardo**, dating back to the 16th century. It was on the top of this tower that bonfires were lit to warn the population that corsairs had landed or that the island had been invaded. To its right, the **Mdina Dungeon** (daily 10am–4.30pm), is anything but dull. It occupies a real dungeon and offers a grisly trawl through the horrors of sickness, death, torture and executions that plagued the islands in medieval times. It's best left to sensation-seeking teenagers and is definitely not for young children.

Of a more restful disposition, the **Museum of Natural History** (daily 9am–5pm) is housed in the Palazzo Vilhena, an enchanting old building boasting a delightful courtyard. The original building on this site, destroyed by an earthquake in 1693, was the seat of the Università, Malta's original governing body. Today it covers various topics such as Maltese Geology and Palaeontology, exotic mammals, marine fauna, insects, shells and birds and other topics like human evolution.

TRIQ VILLEGAIGNON

Mdina's main thoroughfare is **Villegaignon Street ❷**, named after the French knight who defended Mdina from the Turks in 1551. Along its length are Malta's finest houses, preserved by the island's ancient families. Many have private art treasures that would be gratefully welcomed by museums in any country.

At the start is the chapel dedicated to St Agatha, built in 1417 and renovated by Lorenzo Gafà in 1694. Opposite is the Casa Inguanez (1350), home of Malta's oldest noble family. To watch the **Mdina Experience** (www.themdinaexperience.com; daily 10am–5pm), a 30-minute audiovisual spectacular retracing Mdina's history, take **Mesquita Street** to the square.

Return to Villegaignon Street and turn left to **St Paul's Square**, the spacious forecourt to Mdina's cathedral but also the Victorian Gothic **Casa Gourgin** and, opposite, the **Banca Giuratale** (now the Magistrates' House), built by Grand Master Vilhena for the Università. During the revolt against the French in 1798, the Banca became the legislative headquarters of the resistance leaders.

Mdina Cathedral
The highlight of St Paul's Square is undoubtedly the **Cathedral of Saint Paul ❸**. Its site is historic: the home of St Publius is reputed to have stood here. And before Roger I, the Norman Count of Sicily, constructed a church here at the beginning of the 12th century, several others had stood there over the centuries. Roger's church was destroyed by the 1693 earthquake that shook the whole of the central Mediterranean. Only the apse at the back of the cathedral survived, a credit to the

Inside St Paul's Cathedral

renowned Maltese architect Lorenzo Gafà who, while working on the cathedral a few years earlier in 1681, had decided to strengthen its structure. When Gafà was again commissioned to design and supervise the new building in 1697, he incorporated the apse into the new structure.

Built in the shape of a Latin cross, the cathedral interior is sumptuous. The memorial tablets in the nave resemble those in St John's in Valletta: both combine the macabre and the angelic in a most dramatic way. Vincenzo and Antonio Manno were commissioned in 1794 to paint the frescoes on the ceiling, featuring scenes from the life of St Paul. In the north transept, look out for Mattia Preti's painting of St Paul saving the Maltese people from Saracen invaders in 1422.

According to local lore, the cathedral's silver processional cross accompanied Godfrey de Bouillon when he entered Jerusalem at the culmination of the First Crusade. In the shrine to the left of the main altar is an icon of the Madonna, reputedly painted by St Luke, but which is more likely to be Byzantine.

The **Cathedral Museum** (Mon–Sat 9.30am–5pm), on the right side of Archbishop's Square, opposite the cathedral's entrance, features a number of items rescued from the 1693 earthquake: 15th-century Sicilian panels that decorated the cathedral's choir, and some superb Dürer woodcuts.

Continue on Mdina's main road to **Palazzo Falson** (www.palazzofalson. com; Tue–Sun 10am–5pm). Originally built in the 14th century, and added to in the 15th century, it has been beautifully restored to reflect the domestic style of Mdina's 16th-century Golden Age. Just opposite stands the Carmelite Priory (Mon–Sat 10am–4pm). The museum inside holds Italian and Maltese paintings, several fine engravings (some produced by Goya), and a comprehensive collection of woodcuts by Albrecht Dürer, although the highlight is definitely the friars' eclectic kitchen and refectory.

THE BASTIONS

As you continue along the road, you'll find a number of unique boutiques – ideal for a spot of gift shopping – and Bastion Square. This is a popular spot for photos thanks to the picturesque houses and the view across most of central Malta from the bastions.

This may be the ideal time to stop for lunch. Walk down the winding alley to the right of Bastion Square all the way to the recently-restored palace, Palazzo de Piro. A grand building, it dates back to the second half of the 16th century and was built by Malta's most revered architect Girolamo Cassar. Today it houses the **Xpresso Café and Bistro**, see ❶, a great spot for a bite either in the open-air courtyard or

Wignacourt Museum display

on the terrace, overlooking the magnificent view.

WALKING TO RABAT

Head back to Mdina Gate and through Howard Gardens, which divides Mdina and Rabat. At the end of Museum Road is the **Domus Romana** ❹ (www.heritagemalta.org; daily 9am–5pm), the most important of the area's Roman remains. Formerly the house of a wealthy citizen, and also known as the Roman Villa Museum, its foundations were discovered in 1881. It contains a fascinating collection of Roman artefacts such as ladies' ornately carved bone hairpins,

weaving bobbins, a bone-carved baby rattle, terracotta theatrical masks, fine tableware and a unique silver ring recovered from the Islamic cemetery nearby.

Just outside the museum, you can hop onto the **Trackless Train** (daily 10am–5pm on the hour), which chugs from here on a 30-minute journey that will delight young travellers and educate those of all ages. It is an alternative to walking around the area, and even passes by the Old Train Station, which harks back to when Malta had a real on-track train over 50 years ago.

RABAT CENTRE

From the Domus Romana take **St Paul's Street** ❺ into Mdina. If you're feeling peckish, stop at **Crystal Palace**, see ❷, a hole-in-the-wall shop that sells Malta's famous street food, *pastizzi*.

Back on the road, return visitors will notice that this stretch has been restored and is now rather pretty – with many of the townhouses along it having been done up or turned into restaurants or cafés. On nearby Parish Square is **St Paul's Church**, founded in 1575, and rebuilt by Lorenzo Gafà following the earthquake of 1693. The church's main altar was designed by Mattia Preti; the painting above it of St Paul's shipwreck is by Stefano Erardi. To the right-hand side of the church sprawls the **Wignacourt Complex** ❻ (www.wignacourtmuseum.com; daily

Knock knock

As you walk through Mdina, look out for unusual doorknockers on the large palazzo doors. Known as 'Il-Habbata' in Maltese, they often reflect the personality and taste of the homeowner. The most popular ones include lions' heads, seahorses or dolphins, while others represent the family's coat of arms. Most commonly made from brass, the doorknocker entered the island's architectural history many years back as a matter of necessity. However it has survived the mechanical and electric doorbell to become part of Malta's iconic street embellishment.

Picturesque Mdina   *St Agatha's Catacombs*

9.30am–5pm), which incorporates St Paul's Grotto, catacombs, World War II shelters and the Wignacourt Museum. St Paul's Grotto is said to be where St Paul lived for the three months he spent on Malta, while the catacombs are a warren of burial chambers waiting to be explored. The museum is less enticing, but holds paintings by European artists dating back to the 16th century.

If you want to visit more catacombs, then a few minutes' walk along the road are the extensive **St Agatha's Catacombs** (Mon–Fri 9am–5pm, Sat 9am–2pm). Local lore says that St Agatha was in Malta and hid in Rabat's catacombs but later returned home to Sicily only to be tortured and die a martyr rather than marry the Roman governor of Catania. The highlights here are its many superbly coloured frescoes, most of which are medieval, but some date to before the Arab invasion. Sadly all have been defaced. Be warned that the tunnels are very dark – it's a good idea to bring a torch.

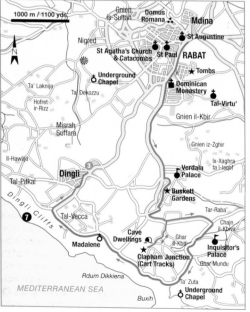

DINGLI

It's a good 30-minute walk from the centre of Rabat out to Dingli, but it is a pleasant one. If you'd rather not walk, then hop on the 56 bus, which will take you straight to Dingli.

Dingli is a rural area and one of the largest stretches of countryside in Malta – it's a haven for those keen to break away from the hustle and bustle for a few hours.

If you are walking on the main road from Rabat, you will pass by **Verdala Castle**. It was built in 1586 during the

Dingli Cliffs, Malta's highest point

reign of Hugues Loubenx de Verdalle and now serves as the official summer residence of the President of Malta, but isn't open to the public.

Further along the same road you will find the hill down to **Buskett**, the only woodland area in Malta, set in the lush valley of Wied Il-Luq, south of Rabat and east of Dingli. Buskett Gardens were planted by the Knights of Malta to be used as a hunting ground. Today the gardens are home to orange trees, cacti, Mediterranean pines and cypress trees, and a variety of shrubs and flowers. It is the perfect place for an afternoon walk or picnic.

The road out of Buskett leads to Dingli, a charming little village, with its pretty square and authentic cafés. It is **Dingli Cliffs** ❼, though, Malta's highest point, that is the main attraction here. Aside from the lovely walks, you'll enjoy open sea views over the tiny, uninhabited isle of Filfla, as well as inland to Buskett Gardens and Verdala Palace. This is no doubt one of the best places on the island to watch the sun set.

After sunset, the perfect way to end this route is to go for an early dinner at **Diar il-Bniet**, see ❸, which celebrates local cuisine and produce.

Food and drink

❶ XPRESSO CAFÉ AND BISTRO

3 Bastion Street, Mdina; tel: 2010 0560; www.palazzodepiro.com; daily 9.30am–10pm; €€€

Dine in grand surroundings indoors, or outside enjoying the panoramic views across Malta. The food is fresh and creative, making use of local, in-season ingredients at every opportunity.

❷ CRYSTAL PALACE

St Paul's Street, Rabat; tel: 2145 3323; daily; €

You may have heard of *pastizzi* – the Maltese street food delicacy made from filo pastry parcels, stuffed with ricotta cheese or peas. They may not be very healthy but they are moreish, and this little café is considered to be the very best place to try them. Here you'll get to mingle with locals at all hours of the day and night – Crystal Palace is especially popular with clubbers on their way home after a night out.

❸ DIAR IL-BNIET

Main Street, Dingli; tel; 2762 0727; www.diarilbniet.com; Mon, Tue, Thu–Sat 10.30am–11pm, Sun 9.30am–7pm, Wed 10.30am–5pm; €€

Run by two charming sisters, the seasonal menu offers traditional Maltese delicacies – from cakes and bakes, to platters and stews. This is one of Malta's only genuine agritourism experiences. The adjacent shop is stocked with fresh vegetables, fruit, herbs and flowers all picked from their farm.

Bugibba seafront

QAWRA, BUGIBBA AND ST PAUL'S BAY

Although very touristy, this part of the island promises some fantastic family activities, top restaurants and a lively nightlife. While St Paul's Bay still harks back to its roots as a quiet fishing village, Bugibba and Qawra have both become busy entertainment spots.

DISTANCE: 5km (3 miles)
TIME: Half day or evening
START: St Paul's Bay
END: Qawra
POINTS TO NOTE: By day this is a popular spot for swimming in the sea, and each of the many lidos here has watersports facilities. By night it becomes loud and brash, attracting a young crowd eager for a good night out, so do bear that in mind if you fancy something more low-key.

The Aquarium at Bugibba

What began as a tiny fishing village hundreds of years ago has now become one of Malta's largest districts, with nearly 15,000 inhabitants. Situated just a short walk from the sea, this whole area – namely St Paul's Bay, Qawra and Bugibba – becomes host to some 60,000 people in the summer, when locals flock here for a seaside retreat. All three towns are conveniently located along one long promenade strollable in an hour or two.

ST PAUL'S BAY

Starting at the **St Paul's Bay ❶** end of the promenade eases you in gently to this bustling area – which gets busier the further along you go.

St Paul's Bay is still the most traditional of the three towns; it was named after St Paul, who was shipwrecked nearby while travelling to Rome. If time allows, you could take a boat over to St Paul's Island – the exact spot where St Paul is believed to have been shipwrecked – to visit the St Paul's Statue, erected in 1845. While there isn't much to do in the area, there are a number of

St Paul's Island, the site of the Apostle's legendary shipwreck

boutiques to explore and some cafés to have breakfast or brunch in. That said, the best restaurant in the area has to be **Tarragon ❶**, which only opens for dinner (or for Sunday lunch); so it makes sense to come back later in the day.

BUGIBBA

Sometimes referred to as a 'mini Blackpool', **Bugibba ❷** is busy, touristy and full of life long into the night. It is very popular with families, who find there is something here to please all ages, including bumper cars, dodgems, trampolines and a small waterpark. To make the most of the atmosphere, grab an ice-cream at **Sottozero ❷** and amble along the promenade at a leisurely pace. There's plenty for adults too, including cinemas, bingo halls, karaoke, clubs and a large casino.

Further inland, you'll find an endless array of non-Maltese restaurants including British-style pubs, and Chinese and Indian eateries.

QAWRA

Much like Bugibba, **Qawra ❸** is an hedonistic hotspot. Slightly more laid-

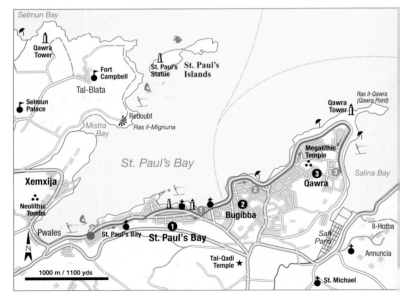

The glass-roofed tunnel at Malta National Aquarium

back and traditional than Bugibba (although just a five-minute walk away), it tends to attract many locals – thanks largely to the many good-value restaurants here.

As you continue along the promenade you will pass the **Aquarium**, several hotels and many restaurants, all vying for your custom. Locals are more likely to want to hang out on the beach, and you will spot them setting up picnics on the coast – a good idea if you have the provisions. Alternatively, if it's a delicious sit-down meal you're after walk right along the promenade to **Duo** ❸ and its top-quality cuisine, a rarity amongst a cluster of non-descript restaurants.

The aquarium

One of the best family destinations on the island is the Malta National Aquarium (daily 10am–8pm), situated midway on the Bugibba/Qawra promenade. Opened in 2013 and popular ever since, it has also become a leading entity for the preservation of marine life and its environment. The tanks here house an impressive collection of fish and sharks, as well as a glass-roofed tunnel so you can see the fish swim all around you. While there's a charge to enter the aquarium, the nearby playground – one of the best on the island – is free.

Food and drink

❶ TARRAGON

Church Street, St Paul's Bay; tel: 2157 3759; Mon–Sat 6.30–11pm, Sat until 12.30am, Sun noon–3.30pm; €€€€
Smart and inviting, food is considered 'art' at Tarragon – which is run by well-known local chef, Marvin Gauci. Blending traits of molecular gastronomy with renowned Mediterranean flavours, you'll find a menu of juicy steaks, the freshest fish and irresistible desserts.

❷ SOTTOZERO

Spring Street, corner with St Anthony Street, Bugibba; tel 7906 9266; www.

sottozerofactory.com; daily 10–2am; €
Arguably the best ice-cream shop on the island, you'll find everything here from the best scoop of chocolate, to a cup of vegan vanilla. The choice is endless and the price is right.

❸ DUO

3, Qawra Coast Road; tel: 2157 8236; www.duomalta.com; Mon–Sun noon–4pm, 6.30–11pm, with exceptions; €€€
Healthy and enticing, you're sure to find something on the menu to fall in love with at Duo. Reflecting a broad spectrum of Mediterranean gastronomy, the pace here is relaxed and the food is made for sharing (that is, if you want to!).

MALTA'S TAIL - THE NORTH

Picturesque and open, the north is renowned for its sprawling countryside, beautiful sandy beaches and excellent selection of bars and restaurants. It gets very busy during the summer, when locals flock here to their summer residences, but it is very tranquil in the winter.

DISTANCE: 11km (6.8 miles)
TIME: Full day
START: Golden Bay
END: Mellieha
POINTS TO NOTE: Buses, although regular from Valletta and other parts of the island, can be limiting if you plan to beach hop. It is best to hire a car or scooter to explore this area of Malta. Weather-wise, the north can get especially windy, even during the hottest periods. This can mask just how strong the sun is, so be sure to slather on the sun cream. Sun beds and umbrellas should be available for hire on all the beaches, especially during the summertime. The north of Malta is also a marine protected area and has some excellent diving sites and diving schools.

The north is home to four of Malta's best beaches, as well as the pretty town of Mellieha, which has become a bit of a foodie hotspot. If you fancy beach hopping, this route highlights the best on offer. Alternatively, find your favourite and stick with it; it really is hard to beat a lazy day on a Mediterranean beach.

GOLDEN BAY

Golden Bay ❶ is one of the island's most picturesque beaches and it even boasts a 'Beach of Quality' accolade. Make sure to get here really early to make the most of your time – and to secure a good spot on the sand, especially during the summer months. Set in an area of rare natural beauty, Golden Bay offers everything you need for an enjoyable day at the beach – cafés and restaurants, sun bed and umbrella hire, and plenty of fun water sport activities. This is also a fantastic beach for families as the water is shallow, although it's important to keep an eye on the currents, as it can get rough in places.

GHAJN TUFFIEHA

Heading up the hill from Golden Bay, a 10-minute walk along the coast and

Popular Għajn Tuffieħa

a left turn take you to popular **Għajn Tuffieħa ❷**, aptly named Riviera by the locals.

But access to this beach paradise isn't easy: you'll have to walk down the very long flight of steep steps (and, of course, back up again) but it is definitely worth it – especially as it is usually far less busy than Golden Bay. The setting is almost completely free from any kind of development. It is best to pack a picnic when travelling here, as facilities are limited.

Għajn Tuffieħa boasts a Blue Flag so be assured that the water quality, environment management and safety checks are all topnotch.

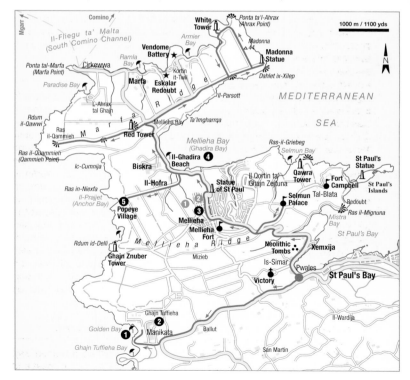

Admiring the rocky shore

MELLIEHA

As the morning comes to an end, head to **Mellieha** ❸, the biggest town in this part of the island. As you drive up through Xemxija Bay, you can't miss the **Selmun Palace**, an 18th-century fortress designed by Domenico Cachia, round the bend near the summit of the first hill. Nearby Selmun Bay is a little slice of paradise – if you can reach it (the access is by an arduous trek).

Back on the coastal road, continue to the roundabout, take the exit marked **Mellieha Centre** and drive through the town.

Take the first left around the base of **Mellieha Church** and park at the top of the hill near the cemetery and

Mellieha Church

children's playground. You might want to take a stroll, see the local sights and absorb the atmosphere, then rest your feet up at the **Sea View Café and bar** ❶, a wonderful place for a drink or lunch. From the terrace of the small bar, there is a panoramic view of Mellieha Bay spreading out below with the White Tower on Marfa Ridge clearly visible.

Walk back to see **Our Lady Chapel**, one of the island's oldest, most venerated ecclesiastical institutions. Not only was it hewn from a rock but, according to local legend, it was the site of St Paul's prayers after he was shipwrecked not far from the island's coastline. Though the chapel is modest in size, there are, on the upper walls and the roof, some particularly lovely frescoes dating back to the 11th century.

Return to your car and the main road for the drive to Malta's 'tail'. Head left down the hill, past the crescent-shaped, sandy **Ghadira Bay** ❹, one of Malta's largest and most popular. Be warned that the road behind it is invariably crowded in high summer. Families flock here because the waters are considered to be among the safest and there are excellent facilities for children, including bouncy castles and slides out on the water.

If you prefer to enjoy the natural beauty of the area, visit the Bird Sanctuary behind the beach – a fresh water

Popeye Village

The Red Tower, also called St Agatha's Tower

haven for migrating birds. Alternatively, climb the hill towards the **Red Tower Fortress** (daily 10am–4pm) at the top, which was built by the Knights in 1647. To explore the area on foot, take the part-dirt road past the tower to **Ras il-Qammieh** at the south of the tail.

MARFA RIDGE

To reach the tail's north end, return to the main road and take the road opposite, which runs along the top of **Marfa Ridge** with Mellieha Bay below on the right. This is a popular summer resort for islanders, and from the cliffs you'll see many anchored boats, with their occupants picnicking or swimming off the nearby rocks. Several roads lead the other way off this main route – but none interconnect, so you must retrace your steps to the main road – including the one to Armier, which hosts great *festa* cel-

ebrations. At **Dahlet ix-Xilep** there's a small statue of the Madonna and a Lady Chapel, from which the **White Tower** is a 15–20 minute walk away.

POPEYE VILLAGE

Return to the main road, and Ghadira, following the signposts to **Popeye Village** ❺ (daily 9.30am–5.30pm, July–Aug until 7pm), which was built for the 1980 movie starring the late Robin Williams. Today it is a big draw for families, who can explore the old set, relax on the beach, take a boat trip out to see the bay, or shop for souvenirs.

It's now time for dinner, so return the way you came and head back to Mellieha. The town has been named a European Destination of Excellence for its facilities. These include superb restaurants which attract locals and visitors from across the islands, notably the traditional **Giuseppe's** ❷.

Food and drink

❶ SEA VIEW CAFÉ AND BAR

Triq Salvinu Vella, Mellieha; tel: 9928 7539; https://seaviewcafemellieha.business.site; daily 9am–11pm; €€
It is the view that's hard to beat here, although the food is also excellent. Wraps, sandwiches, pies and Maltese specials are the order of the day, followed by a slice of cake.

❷ GIUSEPPE'S

Gorg Borg Olivier Street; tel: 2157 4882; www.giuseppismalta.com; Mon–Sat noon–3.30pm, 7.30–10pm, Sun 12.30–3.30pm; €€€€
Run by talented chef patron Michael Diacono, who comes from one of the island's most famous foodie families, Giuseppe's never fails to disappoint. The mostly Maltese menu changes seasonally and uses the freshest produce.

The citadel rises above the town

VICTORIA, GOZO

Gozo's historical capital may be pint-sized, but it's got plenty to offer, including a busy market, fantastic shops and the stunning Citadel.

DISTANCE: 5km (2.4 miles)
TIME: Half day
START: Victoria
END: Victoria
POINTS TO NOTE: To get to Victoria by bus, take the 301 from Mgarr on the mainland. This will drop you off in the main square – the perfect place to start your journey round the capital. Unlike in the past, ferries back to Malta now run through the night, although they become much less frequent after 11pm.

The Knights of St John treated Malta and Gozo with the same care. But Gozo had none of Malta's natural defences, and was, thus, particularly vulnerable to both piracy and foreign invasion. In 1551 there was precious little protection against marauding Ottomans who ransacked the island. Gozo had a short period of independence (1798–1800) when Malta was ruled by the French. Under the British, Malta and Gozo were reunited; Queen

Victoria gave her name to Gozo's capital and elevated it to city status as part of her Golden Jubilee celebrations in 1887. It later became known by its ancient name Rabat ('suburb'). Both names are now used.

THE MAIN SQUARE

If driving, there is parking in Victoria behind the bus depot but be warned that most spaces are gone by 9.30am. If you haven't had breakfast at your hotel, then be tempted by the home-made pastries and good service at **Bellusa Café** ①.

Pjazza Indipendenza ① (known locally as It-Tokk) is a World War II memorial. The other monumental building is the **Banca Giuratale**, erected in 1733 by Grand Master Vilhena.

To enter the maze of little streets and alleys that is **Il Borgo**, the old part of the town, take the short street by **Gangu's Bar**. During the week the street hosts a small vegetable market – the ideal place to pick up foodie

Shopping for souvenirs

Façade of the cathedral in Victoria's Cathedral Square

souvenirs to take home. The nearby **Ginevra** is also popular with locals.

St George's Square ② lies at the end, dominated by the magnificent facade of the eponymous Baroque church. Built in 1678 in the shape of a cross, it is a seamless mixture of old and new. The striking bronze altar canopy, executed in 1967, is a copy of the one Bernini carved for St Peter's in Rome. The main altarpiece, a glowing triumphant St George, was painted by Mattia Pretti (1613–99), of Valletta cathedral fame.

THE BACKSTREETS

To the right of the church, St George Street is a winding, meandering road lined by small shops and old houses. Note the balconies and the doors painted in a shade known as Gozo green. At the first T-junction, take a right and an almost immediate left. At a junction with a large statue of St George on the corner building, go left, and the street shortly opens onto **Piazza Santu Wistin**. The south side of this square is terraced with beautiful, two-storey, quin-

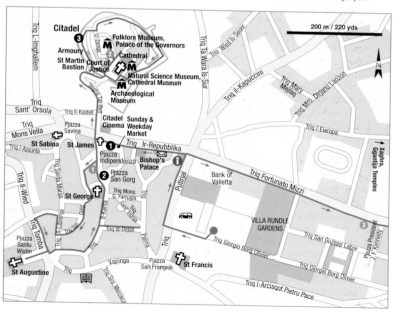

Archaeological Museum exhibits

tessential Gozitan residences, each with an enclosed balcony above the central door. At the far end of the square is the 19th-century **Church of St Augustine**.

Retrace your steps and take a right on **Triq Il-Karita**, then a left at the first T-junction up School Street. Next up is a particularly timeless part of Victoria. Look out for a statue of the Madonna and Child accepting bread rolls from a kneeling supplicant. Then on the right is **Narrow Street**, a long courtyard where you'll encounter women working on their lace patterns and children playing. If it weren't for the electric wires running overhead, you could be in another century.

THE CITADEL

Retrace your steps back to top of the street and turn right. The road opposite St James's Church leads straight up to the **Citadel ❸**; climb to the tree-shaded terrace opposite for a view of the massive fortifications and the cathedral. In the citadel's **Pjazza Katidral** are three main buildings: the cathedral takes centre stage; to its left, in the 17th-century **Palace of the Governors** are the law courts; to the right are the **Chapter Hall**, which dates back to 1899, and the **Bishop's Palace** which, until 1551, was a residence of the *hakim* (Muslim governor) of Gozo.

The cathedral
The Church of the Assumption, better known as the **cathedral** and designed by Lorenzo Gafà, was built between 1697 and 1711 on the site of a temple dedicated to Juno. It has Gafà's usual lightness and grace, but because funds ran dry, the dome he intended for it was never completed. This deficiency has cleverly been turned into an asset by a trompe-l'oeil substitute, painted by Antonio Manuele of Messina in 1739.

The Citadel museums
Before taking a walk around the bastions, you might want to spend some time in the citadel's small museums.

The excellent **Folklore Museum** (daily 9am–5pm) off Triq Il-Fosse spreads over three 16th-century houses. As an architectural group they are unique in the Maltese islands, admired for the simple delicacy of the stonework and their 'Norman' windows. Don't be deterred by the folklore label; the collection is a fascinating look at rural Gozitan life and its bygone times.

The **Old Prison** (daily 9am–5pm) showcases the most extensive collection of historical graffiti on the island. The inmates, incarcerated in the tiny cells here between around 1600 and the 1880s, left poignant carvings of ships, names, dates, games and human figures.

The **Archaeological Museum** (daily 9am–5pm) is reached through the small arch to the right of the cathedral square in Palazzo Bondi. The exhibits range from Neolithic to Medieval, and among them the 12th-century tomb-

The view from the bastions

stone of a young Muslim girl, Majmuna, is particularly touching.

The bastions

Walk round the bastions in a clockwise direction; a set of steps leads to a walkway across the top of the citadel's entrance, with the best views over the piazza. Continuing along the bastions, climb the steps to **St Martin's Cavalier**; to the right are the ruins of buildings destroyed in the earthquake of 1693. The walkway starts to curve and the wall blocks the view, until you reach the telescope. Here look out for the Cross of St Joseph; you can distinguish Marsalforn, the fishing village and popular beach resort, behind it. If you are ready for lunch at this point head to **Ta' Rikardu** ❷ to enjoy some traditional fare.

Take the long flight of steps down to the rear of the citadel, where the walls' full thickness can be fully appreciated. You walk through the lower part and its narrow streets edged by high walls and ruins. To reach the bus terminus or car park, head to Republic Street and retrace your steps.

Just down the main road, you'll find the more commercial part of Victoria, as well as the **Villa Rundle Gardens**, originally planted under British rule in 1914. **Arkadia Shopping Centre**, on the left, houses all sorts of high street shops, as well as a large supermarket, which will come in handy if you're staying at a self-catering farmhouse locally. Just opposite, **Mojo's** ❸ serves up delicious fresh salads and juices.

From here it's a five-minute drive or 20-minute bus ride back to the ferry terminal.

Food and drink

❶ BELLUSA CAFÉ

34, Independence Square; tel: 2155 6243; daily 7am–7pm; €

This has been a popular choice for over 50 years with Gozitans. The homemade omelettes will get your day off to a great start.

❷ TA' RIKARDU

Fosos Street, the Citadel; tel: 2155 2953; daily 11am–7pm; €€

This is about as authentic as it gets. Even though prices here have been steadily rising, this is still the best place for really Gozitan fare, including their signature platter and bread and goats' cheese combo.

❸ MOJO'S

Kennedy Square, Rabat; tel: 2156 9596; Mon–Sat 8am–3.45pm, Sun 10.30am–3.45pm; €€

The informal atmosphere at this café makes it a firm favourite. Their healthy and creative salads are a must, although their less-than-healthy burger will probably tempt you if you're really hungry.

ROUND GOZO

This tiny island includes the world's oldest free-standing temple, unspoilt villages and near-biblical landscapes. This criss-crossing route will provide you with a flavour of Gozitan life: its beaches, countryside, historical treasures and food.

> **DISTANCE:** 20 (12.4 miles)
> **TIME:** Full day and evening
> **START:** Mgarr Harbour
> **END:** Mgarr Harbour
> **POINTS TO NOTE:** The crossing to Gozo is easy. The car ferry leaves Cirkewwa, in the very north of Malta, every 45 minutes and the crossing takes 25 minutes. Gozo is actually better sign-posted than Malta, so it's quite easy to find your way round. Though the bus service is efficient, a hire car will give you the freedom to explore in your own time and at your own pace. This route is designed to avoid Victoria, but head for it if you get lost.

Gozo may only be a 25-minute ferry ride away from Malta, but as you step off the boat here you immediately feel the difference. While the topography is pretty similar to its larger sister island, Gozo feels less built up and more rural, which in turn makes it more laid back and traditional.

Leaving **Mgarr Harbour** ❶, take the road to **Nadur**. Driving towards the town, you will notice the windmills to your right, in Qala. These are among the last remaining windmills of the many that once dotted the countryside.

The church of **Saints Peter and Paul**, built in 1760, dominates Nadur's main square. Drive north from the church square and at Triq Dicembru 13, take a left. Turn left again at the first T-junction, then right at the following T-junction. Look for signs to **San Blas Bay** and **Dahlet Qorrot**. At the first fork, go left to San Blas Bay if you don't mind a steep walk from the parking area to the beach. For the gentler option, take the right turn to the old fishing harbour of Dahlet Qorrot. There are concrete steps that lead to the upper cliff, where you can walk (with a good local map). Alternatively you might try the more precarious lower path at the water's edge. San Blas is a delightful little cove with just enough sand for a few families to share, so try to get there early.

Leaving San Blas, take the road back to Nadur, but at the first T-junction go right towards Ramla. At the second T-junction head towards Victoria, and at the next junction follow the sign to Ramla once again. Halfway down the road is a small

Ggantija Temples, with Victoria in the background

ookout with spectacular views of the valley with its terraced fields of fig and orange trees (screens made from local bamboo protect the crops from the wind).

RAMLA BAY

Ramla Bay ❷ is Gozo's longest and finest beach. In the summer, stake out an early claim to be assured of a space. The shortcut to **Calypso's Cave** (avoiding Xaghra) is easily missed: about 30 metres (100ft) beyond the small police station, a steep, single-lane gravel road bears to the right. If the shortcut looks too daunting, follow the signs to Xaghra, where directions to Calypso's Cave are clearly posted. The cave is not much more than a narrow, rocky slit but it is here, if we are to believe local legend, and the works of Homer, that the Greek hero Odysseus (Ulysses to the Romans) was washed ashore and into the arms of the golden-haired temptress, Calypso, on his epic return from Troy. It is said that Calypso wished to detain Odysseus on the island and make him her immortal husband, but after a number of years, Odysseus returned home to his wife Penelope. The cave is currently inaccessible to the public due to geological movement but the views of Ramla Bay here are excellent.

Xaghra is also home to the Unesco-listed **Ggantija Temples ❸** (daily 9am–4.30pm) – the most famous and best-preserved of all the prehistoric temples on the Maltese Islands. Constructed from 3600–3000BC, this is the oldest free-standing stone building known to man, predating Egypt's pyramids and Britain's Stonehenge by over 1,000 years. The two temples cover 1,000 sq metres (10,800 sq ft), and their astonishing rear wall still rises 6 metres (20ft) and contains megaliths weighing in at 40–50 tons – the most gigantic blocks used in any of the archipelago's herculean structures. Entrance to the temples is from a newly constructed Interpretation Centre that provides an introduction to life in Neolithic times.

MARSALFORN

Leaving the temples, take the main road to Xaghra, and at the first T-junction go right. The road to **Marsalforn** is well-marked. This seaside resort is popular with locals and tourists, who have a choice between rock, shingle and sand beaches. Even at the height of the season in July and August, it is worth braving the crowds to lunch at **Kartell ❶**.

Round the bay from Marsalforn, you'll find Gozo's famous **salt pans**, simply follow the road that runs parallel to Marsalforn's waterfront. Take the first right turn; just before the quay, a road swings left up the hill leading to the upper promenade, follow the road as it leads under a sandstone cliff (water will lap at your wheels), and around the next bend are the salt pans – shallow pools cut from the soft coastal rock. Although Gozo now imports all the salt it needs, many people still collect it here each September.

Sandstone cliffs at Marsalforn

TA' PINU

From the pans, beyond the overhang, a right leads to **Zebbug**. This charm-

ing village occupies the top of a ridge from which there are wonderful views of the island. After a climb in first gear, the first flat area is the church-fronted **main**

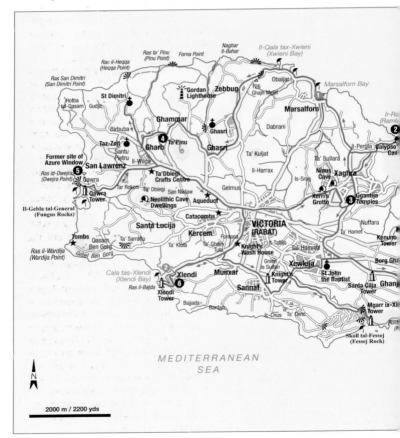

The salt pans used to harvest sea salt

square. For the best view over the island, leave as though heading for Victoria, but shortly after the road forks left take an immediate right, followed by a left. The road continues past a school into a rest stop with benches and a car park.

To avoid Victoria, go down the hill at the far end of the viewing area, and at the cemetery take the gravel road which branches off to the right. It's not sign-posted, but eventually you'll arrive in **Ghasri**. This is old Gozo, where farm-houses have not been prettified.

The road at the right of the church runs through **Ghammar** and to the shrine church of **Ta' Pinu ❹**. In the late 19th century a sick woman was believed to have been cured after her son heard a voice in the Ta' Pinu chapel, and from then on the little chapel became a place of pilgrimage. To accommodate the thousands of devotees, a huge neo-Roman-esque church was built in the 1920s, though the original 16th-century chapel is tucked into it, behind the main altar. A room to the right of the Lady Chapel is filled with discarded crutches and leg braces, baby clothes that poignantly attest to cures and escapes from peril.

Leaving Ta' Pinu, take the road to Victoria, then turn left at the Gharb sign. As you enter the town, keep an eye open for the controversial church facade: some believe that this 17th-century architectural gem is nothing more than a copy of Francesco Borromini's Sant'Agnes in Rome's Piazza Navona, others claim that it is original. Either way, the exterior is a delight. Inside, the church is smaller than expected, but it's a splendidly ornate Baroque structure. In the square, the **Market Cross** is one of the finest on the island.

MEDITERRANEAN SEA

ta' San Blas (Blas Bay)
Mistra Rocks
Dahlet Qorrot
emma
Ta' Cini
Qala
Menhir
Wardija
Hondoq ir-Rummien
Il-Qasam
Ghar Dorf
Redoubt
Ras il-Qala (Qala Point)
Gebel tal-Halfa
Il-Hneijja
nla tal-Mgarr arr Harbour)
Il-Fliegu ta' Ghawdex (North Comino Channel)
Santa Marija Bay
Bejn-il-Kniemen (Blue Lagoon)
Annunciation
Cominotto (Kemmunett)
Comino (Kemmuna)
Santa Marija Tower
Redoubt
Ras l-Irqieqa
Il-Fliegu ta' Malta (South Comino Channel)
Sliema, Valletta
Cirkewwa
Cirkewwa

Ta' Pinu shrine

DWEJRA AND THE INLAND SEA

Drive through Gharb and take the narrow road to **San Dimitri**, with its small chapel. This typical stretch of Gozitan countryside leads to a rock escarpment and a coast that looks towards Sicily. Legend has it that in the 16th century, invading Turks kidnapped a Gozitan youth. After his mother prayed to San Dimitri for his return, the youth was whisked off the Turkish galley and back to land. On stormy nights, San Dimitri's lantern is said to glow in the sea, as it did when the saint guided the son back to shore. On the road back to Gharb, look out for **Il-Fanal ta' Gordan**, a lighthouse whose panning beacon can be seen from Malta's north coast at night.

When the road from Gharb takes a right near San Lawrenz en route to Dwejra, look out for the **Gozo Glassblowing Centre**. A little way further on is the **Ta' Dbiegi Crafts Centre** selling pottery.

As you drive downhill to **Dwejra Bay**, Wied Ilma is to the left, and beyond it, the scars of the sandstone quarries. Stop near **Qawra Tower**, which you can climb for sweeping views of the bay. To the left you will see **Fungus Rock**, once highly prized by the Knights for the odd red plant that grows on top of it which was reputed to have miraculous healing powers. To the right used to stand the **Azure Window ❺**, a stunning natural rock arch which has become a popular dive site since its collapse.

To your right you'll see a little road leading down to the **Inland Sea**, a crater into which the sea flows through a cavernous fissure in the cliffs. Little boats sail through the gap on sightseeing trips into the caves and out into the open water, where you'll have an amazing view.

XLENDI

To get to **Xlendi ❻** you cannot avoid Victoria, but at least you can bypass the centre and the route is well signposted. On Victoria's Xlendi side, you'll spot a cavernous 17th-century public **washhouse**, still used by the locals. From here, Xlendi is about 2km (1 mile) away. Park in the car park behind the row of buildings that fronts the bay, or take the road on the left up towards the apartment complexes and park at the top of the bluff. The hillside has been landscaped down to the water, each level connected by steps and walkways. Swimming from the rocks is popular and you might see divers preparing for underwater explorations.

A concrete path leads back along an inlet of the bay. Cross the small bridge and walk to the tower on **Ras Il-Bajda**. The sandstone here is smooth enough for sunbathing and, although some of the rocks near the bay's entrance are sharp, the swimming is generally good. The cliffs of Gebel Ben Gorg and Wardija Point stretch toward the northwestern horizon. Heading in the other direction, you can enjoy a seaside walk for several hundred metres before the path ends at the water's edge. Ambitious walkers can hike all the way along the cliff tops to **Ta' Cenc**.

Swimmers at Dwejra Bay

Crafts being made at Ta'Dbiegi

Xlendi is a good place to stop for lunch. **The Boathouse** ❷ restaurant, located right on the edge of the tiny bay.

THE FINAL STRETCH

Next up on this circular route is **Mgarr Ix-Xini**, an ancient port once used by sailors in longboats and galleys for repairs and rest. To bypass Victoria, retrace your steps from Xlendi as far as the concrete bus shelter, where an extremely sharp right, signed **Munxar**, takes you through that town and toward **Sannat**. Once there, take the road that swings round the left of the church. Within a minute or so, a green-edged sign points left to Mgarr Ix-Xini. Where the hill is at its lowest, a single-lane road veers to the right. The small fishing harbour is well off the tourist track, although it gained notoriety when Brad Pitt and Angelina Jolie used it as the backdrop for their film *By the Sea* (2015).

To get to the domed church of St John the Baptist in **Xewkija**, return to the main road, take a right and at the next T-junction turn right again (Mgarr is signposted). This road leads to the church – a modern building of staggering dimensions. The 75-metre (250ft-) high dome, with a circumference of 85 metres (275ft), is one of the four largest in Europe. The remains of the original 1665 church are through a door on the left of the main altar.

To get the Malta ferry, return to the main road, following signs to Mgarr. Consider having dinner here; **Tmun Mgarr** ❸ is a lively restaurant loved by locals.

Food and drink

❶ KARTELL

Marina Street, Marsalforn; tel: 2155 6918; www.kartellrestaurant.com; daily in summer 11.30am–3pm, 6–10pm (Thu–Tue in winter); €€€€

Locals will leave Malta for the day especially to have lunch here at Kartell; it's an institution. Fish is the speciality, although the vast menu has something for everyone. There is a focus on genuine Gozitan produce and hospitality.

❷ THE BOATHOUSE

Xlendi Seafront; tel 2156 9153; www.theboathousegozo.com; daily noon– 10.30pm; €€€

You're assured of delicious Mediterranean cuisine and something for everyone, from pizzas and pasta, to perfectly-cooked meats and the freshest fish. The desserts are all homemade and worth leaving room for.

❸ TMUN MGARR

Martinu Garces Street, Mgarr; tel: 2156 6276; www.tmunmgarr.com; daily 6.30– 10pm, Fri–Mon also from noon–2pm; €€€

Literally a few minutes' walk from the boat, this restaurant is run by husband-and-wife team Leli and Jane, who give every single dish their love and attention. Their signature pistachio parfait is an absolute must.

COMINO

The largely uninhabited island of Comino makes for a wonderful day trip with its cluster of secret beaches and historic sites. The highlight, the world-famous Blue Lagoon, gets extremely busy in the summer but the magical turquoise waters are a truly unmissable experience.

DISTANCE: 7km (4.3 miles)
TIME: Half or full day
START: Blue Lagoon
END: Blue Lagoon
POINTS TO NOTE: Buses 41 and 42 run from Valletta to Cirkewwa, from where you board the ferry to Comino. Although a number of kiosks set up on Comino in summer, there is only one hotel-restaurant, so it makes sense to pack a picnic. Facilities for families are also limited. Comino gets very busy in summer so it is best enjoyed in spring and autumn, or on dry winter days. Be sure to check the time for the last ferry back.

If Malta is the busy island, and Gozo the quiet island, then Comino is surely the great escape island, where relaxation and sports are the only staple items on the menu. Lying midway between Malta and Gozo, Comino is all of 2.5 sq km (1 sq mile) in size. It takes about 20 minutes to get to Comino by boat.

The name Comino derives from the cumin spice which used to be grown in large quantities here. In fact, it still grows wild in clumps around the island but it is the pink and mauve wild thyme that hits the eye and scents the air when the bees start buzzing to produce what is arguably the region's finest honey.

Throughout the Middle Ages and up until the time of the Knights, both Malta and Gozo were constantly attacked by Saracen pirates, who used Comino as a base from which to assault the islands. Today, Comino is virtually uninhabited.

As you sail towards the island, you'll see the **Santa Marija Tower ❶**, also known as the Comino Tower, erected by the Knights in 1618 for protection against the ever-present threat of an Ottoman invasion. As it turned out, the Turks did not attack so the tower was never put to the test. Now restored, the tower is used as a post for Malta's modest armed forces.

THE BLUE LAGOON

This route starts and finishes at the Blue Lagoon, as it's the only place that the ferryboat berths on the island. Such is the

The heavenly Blue Lagoon

beauty of the lagoon you could choose to spend the whole day here.

The **Blue Lagoon ❷** is a true gem of the Mediterranean, although it is absolutely tiny. The colours of the waters surrounding the island are breathtaking: deep-water indigo and navy, sky and turquoise blue in the sandy bays, peaking to the sparkling azure and emerald of the Blue Lagoon. This is the Mediterranean at its best and there are even playful dolphins that bob up and down in the deep-sea channels between the islands. You can snorkel and swim here in some of the Mediterranean's clearest waters. This little mass of golden sand gets snapped up pretty quickly, especially during the summer months, so it is recommended to head over very early to secure your spot as close to the water as possible.

WALKING ON COMINO

It is worth exploring the rest of Comino. Head for **Santa Marija Bay ❸**, then along the path to the tower to see the ruins of a Knights' quarantine hospital.

From the sea

Sailing around Comino is an exhilarating experience; you can hire a boat, or a yacht if budget allows. This is the ideal way to explore the lesser-known inlets and bays – and avoid the crowds. Try Sailing Charters Malta (tel: 7981 1181) for a private tour, or join a Captain Morgan's good-value full-day cruise (tel: 2346 3333).

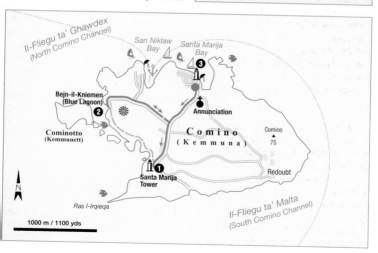

DIRECTORY

Hand-picked hotels and restaurants to suit all budgets and tastes, organised by area, plus select nightlife listings, an alphabetical listing of practical information, a language guide and an overview of the best books and films to give you a flavour of the island.

The Grand Hotel Excelsior

ACCOMMODATION

With tourism being one of the main industries on the island, Malta has a plethora of accommodation options, with prices ranging from cheap to relatively expensive. The choice goes from five-star, luxury hotels in St Julian's and Floriana, and grand hotels in the heart of the island, to centuries-old palaces converted into topnotch designer boutique hotels in Valletta.

Budget travellers will be pleased to know that the renowned Maltese hospitality doesn't limit itself to big spenders. Hostels for students and backpackers are also scattered across the island, with those in Sliema and St Julian's being the most centrally located for the thriving party scene in St Julian's. They are also just a bus-ride away from the capital. Cheaper accommodation on a bed-and-breakfast basis can be found all over the island, including in Sliema and Valletta.

Gozo has a number of hotels, too, including a Kempinski hotel and a number of luxury boutique choices.

These are located in the villages and towns of the island, as well as just outside urban areas. Comino only has one hotel, but it is good value for money.

Agritourism in Malta is still in its infancy, and so far only extends to olive picking, wine tasting and guided tours rather than proper live-ins.

All localities have decent public transport connections and can be reached by taxi.

An extra charge of €0.50 per bed-night is applicable for travellers 18 and over however, the total charge is capped at €5.

Valletta & Floriana

Casa Ellul
81 Old Theatre Street, Valletta; tel: 2122 4821; www.casaellul.com; €€€
Housed within a luxurious, beautifully restored 1830s palazzo, this boutique hotel screams style and sophistication – no wonder it is a favourite with celebrities. There are eight luxurious, individually-designed rooms to choose from.

Grand Hotel Excelsior
Great Siege Road, Floriana; tel: 2125 0520; www.excelsior.com.mt; €€€
Located a stone's throw away from the capital, this large and striking five-star hotel has a stellar reputation. Many of its rooms boast wonderful sea views.

> Price for a double room including breakfast during high season:
> €€€€ = over €300
> €€€ = €180 – 300
> €€ = €80 – 180
> € = under €80

Hotel Phoenicia oozes old-world charm

Hotel Castille

Castille Square, Valletta; tel: 2124 3677; www.hotelcastillemalta.com; €€
Located just 10 feet away from the Office of the Prime Minister, Hotel Castille is a great-value option for those who want to be in the heart of the city, and be easily connected to the rest of the island.

Hotel Phoenicia

The Mall, Floriana; tel: 2122 5241; www. phoeniciamalta.com; €€€€
The 136 room luxury hotel, situated opposite the Renzo Piano-redesigned City Gate, is a local institution that enchants visitors with its old-world charm and elegance.

Luciano Valletta Boutique Hotel

21 Merchant Street, Valletta; tel: 7711 1110; www.vallettaboutique.com; €€
This boutique hotel offers traditionally decorated rooms with rustic stone feature walls and a great location, right in the heart of Valletta, next to St John's Cathedral. Breakfast, cable TV and DVDs are included in the price of the room.

Osborne Hotel

50 South Street, Valletta; tel: 2124 3656; www.osbornehotel.com; €€
This 63 room, three-star hotel is bright and airy, and located just a few metres away from the National Museum of Fine Arts. Its rooms come with flat-screen TVs, large double beds and air-con as standard.

Palazzo Prince d'Orange

St Paul's Street, Valletta; tel: 9912 5200; www.palazzoprincemalta.com; €€€€
No expense was spared when this 17th-century palazzo was renovated into one of Malta's most talked-about boutique hotels. And, if you're looking for a unique place to stay, ask for their Wilhelmina Duplex, overlooking the picture-perfect harbour below.

St Julian's

Boho Hostel

Villa Cycas, Dun Guzeppi Xerri Street; tel: 2765 6008; www.bohohostel.com; €
This hostel has four rooms (one for men, one for women and two mixed), each sleeping six. This is the ultimate place for solo travellers looking for somewhere cheap and decent to sleep.

Cavalieri Art Hotel

Spinola Road, San Giljan; tel: 2318 0000; www.cavalierihotel.com; €€
Located on the water's edge, this establishment is contemporary in style, with an attractive décor and lovely views across to St Julian's Bay. It is very well located if you enjoy being in the thick of things as it is just a short walk from both St Julian's and Sliema.

Corinthia St George's Bay

St George's Bay; tel: 2137 4114; www. corinthia.com; €€€
As one of the first five-star hotels to open in the area, Corinthia San Gorg

Suite at the Corinthia Hotel

has remained a firm favourite with tourists. Facilities include three swimming pools, on-site watersports and diving centres, direct access to a rocky beach, and a spa.

George Hotel
Paceville Avenue; tel: 2011 1000; www. thegeorgemalta.com; €€
Located in the heart of the entertainment district, this hotel is both well-designed and eco-friendly. Each of its 112 rooms is spacious, and comes complete with Wi-Fi, LCD TV and iPhone docking station.

Hilton Malta
Portomaso; tel: 2138 3383; www. hiltonmaltahotel.com; €€
With 410 rooms, the Hilton is one of Malta's largest and most luxurious hotels. The hotel has a number of restaurants, as well as executive lounges, making it a popular choice with business visitors.

Hostel Malti
41 Birkirkara Hill; tel: 2730 2758; www. hostelmalti.com; € (shared rooms available)
Situated in a converted townhouse in Ta' Giorni, neighbouring St Julian's, this hostel is incredibly colourful. It can take up to 32 people and has both shared and private rooms. Ask the owners about kite-surfing opportunities and other fun activities on offer.

Hotel Juliani
25 St George's Road; tel: 2138 8000; www. hoteljuliani.com; €€
Hotel Juliani is located in Spinola Bay, just a five-minute walk to the heart of St Julian's and 20 minutes away from Sliema on foot. Although not technically a boutique hotel, its small size allows for personalised attention.

Hotel Valentina
Dobbie Street; tel: 2138 2232; www. hotelvalentina.com; €€
Centrally located, this modern family-owned hotel has great facilities, including a rooftop pool and bar (both open Apr–Oct), underground car park and free Wi-Fi throughout the hotel. All mod-cons and breakfast is included in the price of the room.

InterContinental Malta
St George's Bay; tel: 2137 7600; www. intercontinental.com/icmalta; €€€
Centrally located, the InterContinental is a quiet retreat just off the St Julian's party-mile. This mammoth establishment of 481 rooms has a stunning Presidential Suite if you're feeling flush.

Le Méridien St Julian's Hotel & Spa
39 Main Street, Balluta Bay; tel: 2311 0000; www.lemeridienmalta.com; €€€€
Overlooking the picturesque promenade separating Sliema and St Julian's, Le Méridien combines the

Pool at the Radisson Blu Resort

charm of a boutique hotel with all the essentials you'd expect from a spa resort. Pets are welcome for a nominal fee.

Marina Hotel Corinthia Beach Resort

St George's Bay; tel: 2370 2000; www. marinahotel.com.mt; €€€

This four-star hotel overlooks the stunning St George's Bay, and its 200 rooms include 11 suites with fabulous views of the sea. Its facilities, including a private pool and bar, will not disappoint.

Radisson Blu Resort St Julian's

St George's Bay, St Julian's; tel: 2137 4894; www.radissonblu.com; €€€

Overlooking the sparkling Mediterranean Sea, the Radisson Blu is the perfect spot for a restful holiday. Stay in one of its 252 stylish rooms and suites, most of which have fabulous sea views.

The Westin Dragonara Resort

Dragonara Road; tel: 2138 1000; www. westinmalta.com; €€

On top of being a splendid hotel, with all the amenities you'd expect from a five-star, the Westin also has a private beach with Blue Flag status.

Sliema & Gzira

Corner Hostel Malta

6 St Margaret Street, Sliema; tel: 2780 2780; www.cornerhostelmalta.com; €

Perfect for budget travellers, this hostel is situated within a restored townhouse, a short walk away from the city centre. There are 12 rooms in total, and guests are free to mingle in the lounge area.

Fortina Spa Resort

Tigné Seafront, Sliema; tel: 2346 2346; www.fortinasparesort.com; €€€

Renowned for its excellent spa facilities, the Fortina also boasts Europe's first-ever therapeutic spa bedrooms, which include two Dermalife Machines for body detoxification, a therapeutic bath and high-pressure massage showers. There are also a number of in-house restaurants to choose from. (Currently closed for renovation, due to reopen June 2020. The Terrace restaurant remains open.)

The Host Guesthouse

Triq L-Imrabat, Sliema; tel: 7988 9339; www.thehostmalta.com; €€

Housed within a traditional property, this five-bedroomed boutique guesthouse offers themed en suite accommodation, and everything you'd expect from the boutique experience: bathrobes, luxurious toiletries and sumptuous breakfasts.

Hostel Jones

Sir Adrian Dingli Street; tel: 9932 0003; www.maltahostel.com; €

This family-owned 6-room, 29-bed hostel is a cheap-yet-chic alternative

to a hotel. This is a place with character – even the walls have been decorated by local artists.

The Palace

High Street, Sliema; tel: 2133 3444; www. thepalacemalta.com; €€

Situated amid Sliema's old townhouses, this exquisite hotel offers spacious rooms including six themed designer suites with names like Light Suite, View Suite, Flavours Suite and Music Suite.

Palazzo Capua

2 Gorg Borg Olivier Street, Sliema; tel: 2133 4711; www.palazzocapuamalta. com; €€€

Some 200 meters/yards from the Sliema seafront Palazzo Capua promises good value in the heart of town, with excellent facilities shared with its neighbouring sister hotel, The Palace.

Preluna Hotel & Spa

124 Tower Road, Sliema; tel: 2133 4001; www.preluna.com; €€

Run by the Preca family for over 40 years, the Preluna is especially popular with expats. To add to its charm, contemporary sea-view rooms are available overlooking the private beach. Restaurants, bars and a fitness suite are all available on site.

The Victoria Hotel

Gorg Borg Olivier Street, Sliema; tel: 2133 4711; www.victoriahotel.com; €€

Well-priced, this hotel is just a stone's throw away from the town centre. The hotel also offers special spa and wellness packages for those looking for total relaxation. Rooms are well equipped and comfortable.

The Waterfront Hotel

The Strand, Gzira; tel: 2090 6899; www. waterfronthotelmalta.com; €€

Enjoying views of the capital's majestic bastions, this hotel is renowned for its personalised hospitality. Most of the 116 rooms have beautiful sea views, and come with a spacious balcony.

Mdina, Rabat & Attard

Chapel 5 Palazzo and Suites

5 Alley 5, St Lucy Street, Naxxar; tel: 7979 3721; www.bedandbreakfast-malta. com; €€

Right in the centre of the historic town of Naxxar, this is a historic and beautifully restored palazzo. Its East-meets-West décor makes for a relaxing retreat where you can enjoy the pool, terraces and even yoga classes. A good choice for those in search of an authentic Maltese experience.

Corinthia Palace Hotel & Spa

De Paule Avenue, Attard; tel: 2144 0301; www.corinthia.com/palace; €€€

As the first Corinthia Hotel to open in the world, this one still retains its old-world charm. The hotel is famous for its attention to detail and person-

alised service, and it's located opposite the San Anton Presidential Palace and Gardens. Pets are welcome.

Point De Vue Guesthouse

2/7 Saqqajja Square, Rabat; tel: 2145 4117; www.pointdevue-mdina.com; €€€€
Located close to the medieval city of Mdina, Point De Vue boasts 12 comfortable rooms with en suite facilities, most of which also enjoy stunning views of the surrounding lush countryside.

The Xara Palace Relais & Châteaux

Misrah il-Kunsill, Mdina; tel: 2145 0560; www.xarapalace.com.mt; €€€€
Set in a palazzo that was once home to a noble Maltese family, the Xara Palace has certainly kept up the luxury and majesty of the building. The rooms are decorated with authentic antiques and most enjoy beautiful views of the surrounding countryside.

Bugibba & Qawra

db San Antonio Hotel & Spa

Tourist Street, Qawra; tel: 2158 3434; www.dbhotelsresorts.com/dbsanantonio; €€€
Newly refurbished, this hotel boasts over 500 rooms and suites, as well as a handful of bars and restaurants where you can enjoy Mediterranean, Indian, Moroccan or Asian cuisines. The outdoor pools overlooking the sea add to the sense of luxury here.

db Seabank Resort + Spa

Marfa Road, Mellieha; tel: 2289 1000; www.dbhotelsresorts.com/dbseabank; €€€
With a large pool, six themed restaurants, three bars, a wellness spa and a range of sports and leisure facilities, this hotel is the ultimate all-in-one-resort. The rooms come with free Wi-Fi, and each has a nautical touch thanks to the blue-and-white décor.

Dolmen Resort Hotel

Dolmen Street, Qawra; tel: 2355 2355; www.dolmen.com.mt; €€€
Thanks to its wide range of facilities which include water sports, a club on the coast, a diving club, a private beach lido, a sauna and a Jacuzzi, the Dolmen resort is a favourite with families.

Maritim Antonin Hotel & Spa Malta

George Borg Olivier Street, Mellieha; tel: 2289 2000; www.martim.com.mt; €€
This four-star hotel has fully-equipped, elegant rooms. The hotel also boasts a rooftop pool, a spa and free Wi-Fi throughout, as well as numerous restaurants, including Les Jardins and The Arches.

Paradise Bay Hotel

Triq Il-Marfa, Mellieha; tel: 2152 1166; www.paradise-bay.com; €€
This popular and spacious hotel is beautifully situated overlooking Mal-

Room at the Pergola Club Hotel and Spa

ta's picturesque sister islands, Gozo and Comino, and is surrounded by the waters of the Mediterranean. It offers practical, well-appointed accommodation, and is very family-friendly.

Pergola Club Hotel and Spa
Adenau Street, Mellieha; tel: 2152 3912; www.pergolahotel.com.mt; €€
All rooms in this four-star hotel are designed with elegance and comfort in mind. Indulge and unwind in their Da Vinci Spa, or take your pick from any one of the five restaurants. There is free Wi-Fi throughout.

Radisson Blu Resort & Spa, Malta Golden Sands
Mellieha; tel: 2356 1000; www.radissonblu.com/goldensandsresort-malta; €€€€
As the top five-star hotel in the area, the Golden Sands has some of the island's most incredible sea views, as well as its own, fully-serviced private beach. Among its many amenities, there are four pools, a diving centre and a spa.

Ramla Bay Resort
Marfa, Mellieha; tel: 2281 2281; www.ramlabayresort.com; €€
Enjoying views of both Gozo and Comino, this hotel has a private sandy beach, a spa, three outdoor pools, one indoor pool, a diving school and a seasonal sports centre. Its landscaped gardens are truly sumptuous.

Soreda Hotel
Andrew Cunningham Street, Qawra; tel: 2157 6267; www.soredahotelmalta.com; €€
This great-value-for-money establishment offers all the amenities of a hotel including an indoor pool and a recently refurbished gym. Types of accommodation here range from standard rooms to self-catering apartments.

Gozo & Comino

Comino Hotel and Bungalows
Comino; tel: 2152 9821; www.cominohotel.com; €€
Situated near San Niklaw Bay on Comino, this hotel has two private sandy beaches and two large swimming pools (one of which is for children). A number of bungalows are also available.

Downtown Hotel
Europe Street, Rabat; tel: 2210 8000; www.downtown.com.mt; €
Situated just a stone's throw away from Rabat's high street, this hotel is fantastic for anyone wishing to explore the island of Gozo. On top of the usual amenities, the hotel also has a bowling alley, once frequented by the Jolie-Pitt family.

Grand Hotel
58 Triq Sant Antnin, Mgarr Harbour; tel: 2216 1000; www.grandhotelmalta.com; €€

The stunning pool at the Kempinski San Lawrenz

Each room at this hotel comes with satellite TV, air-con, an en suite bathroom and free Wi-Fi. If possible, book a room with a sea view to truly delve into the Gozitan way of life.

Hotel Calypso

Marsalforn Bay; tel: 2156 2000; www.hotelcalypsogozo.com; €€

As one of Gozo's most popular hotels, the Calypso has well-sized rooms complete with en suite bathrooms, balcony, a TV set, fridge bar, air-con and Wi-Fi. You can go swimming in Marsalforn Bay just opposite, or in the hotel pool.

Hotel San Andrea

Xatt Ix Xlendi, Munxar; tel: 2156 5555; www.hotelsanandrea.com; €€

This 28-room family-run hotel makes for a wonderful hideaway in pretty Xlendi Bay. The accommodation is comfortable and the facilities good, while meals are served at the award-winning Zafiro Restaurant.

Hotel Ta' Cenc & Spa

Sannat; tel: 2219 1000; www.tacenc.com; €€

Located in a Natura 2000 site (a network of nature protection areas in the EU), away from the hustle and bustle of daily life, this hotel is among Gozo's best and most luxurious, with plenty of countryside to explore. It also has numerous restaurants, including the Carrubo, which is open all year round.

Hotel Xlendi Resort & Spa

St Simon Street, Xlendi; tel: 2755 3719; www.hotelxlendi.com; €

Reasonably priced, this hotel boasts some seriously remarkable views of the glittering Mediterranean Sea. The choice of rooms here varies from self-catering apartments in both standard or sea view deluxe, as well as standard rooms.

Kempinski San Lawrenz Resort

Triq ir-Rokon, San Lawrenz; tel: 2211 0000; www.kempinski.com/gozo; €€€

Situated amid vast gardens, this hotel is the ideal place to leave the world behind and unwind by the pool. The estate also has a spa, an indoor pool, a gym and squash and tennis courts, along with a stunning outdoor pool. Rooms are well decorated in contemporary Italian style and range from studios to three bedroom apartments.

Quaint Boutique Hotel

8, December Street, Nadur, Gozo; tel: 2210 8500; www.quainthotelsgozo.com; €€

Located in the traditional village of Nadur, this is the perfect place to sample 'authentic Gozo'. The 12 rooms have a designer feel to them, and one of the three penthouse suites has a Jacuzzi on the terrace with views of the stunning countryside. Breakfast is served on the ground floor, overlooking one of the town squares.

The popular Café Jubilee

RESTAURANTS

Malta's culinary scene has exploded over the past decade, with new restaurants opening on a monthly basis, even in the most unlikely of places. While Valletta, St Julian's and Sliema remain the most popular destinations for a good meal out, places like Bugibba and Attard are also now meccas for foodies. Gozo also has a surprisingly good restaurant scene, with many locals taking the ferry over just to try out the delicious fare on offer at the various establishments dotted all over the island. This is a place where a restaurant cannot be judged by its frontage or the style of its menu, because authentic Gozitan cuisine doesn't always come in nice packages.

More than ever before, the local restaurant scene has become diversified with a variety of world cuisines on offer: Asian fusion, Mediterranean, Maltese and fine-dining restaurants all operating side-by-side. The sky's the limit, and all budgets are catered for.

Price for two-course meal for one person, including a glass of wine and service
€€€€ = over €50
€€€ = €35–50
€€ = €25–35
€ = under €25

Note that all of the opening times below are subject to change, so it is best to consult each restaurant's website or Facebook page, or to call ahead before visiting.

Valletta & Floriana

Café Jubilee
125 St Lucia Street; tel: 2704 2332; www.cafejubilee.com; daily 8–1am; €
Serving everything from breakfast to after-theatre dinners, this is one of the city's most popular haunts. The eclectic décor accompanies a mostly-Maltese menu. Consult the specials board for the best options.

Da Pippo Trattoria
136 Melita Street; tel: 2124 8029; daily 11.30am–3.30pm; €€
This restaurant has an almost cult status with pasta lovers, who love the concept of sharing from the central pan placed on their table. Also excellent for meat and fish. Lunch only; advance booking required.

The Harbour Club
4/5 Barrierra Wharf; tel: 7922 2332; www.theharbourclubmalta.com; daily 7–10.30pm; €€
A favourite with the 'it' crowd, this restaurant is considered one of the chicest in the capital. The view over the Grand Harbour is magnificent, and

Be sure to try the local seafood

the food and cocktail menu innovative and exciting.

Malata

St George's Square; tel: 2762 2733; daily 11am–3pm and 6pm–midnight; €€€

Possibly one of the most picturesque locations anywhere in Valletta, you can dine al fresco overlooking the dancing fountains of St George's Square. They serve up delicious fantastic French-Maltese cuisine to boot.

Palazzo Preca

54 Strait Street; tel: 2122 6777; www. palazzoprecavalletta.com; Tue–Sat noon–3.30pm and 6.30–10.30pm, Sun 6–10.30pm; €€

Run by a food-mad family, you are assured of a fantastic meal here. The setting is pretty, and the menu varied – fish is their speciality.

Portocinno

8 Boat Street; tel: 7723 5548; https:// porticellomalta.com; daily noon–3pm and 7–11pm; €€€

Right on the seafront near the arrival point for the Sliema–Valletta ferry, this is a lovely spot for a meal. The food is mostly Italian, with fantastic pasta, fish and meat choices.

Rubino

53 Old Bakery Street; tel: 2122 4656; www. rubinomalta.com; Mon–Fri 12.30–2.30pm, Tue–Sat 7.30–10.30pm; €€€

This was one of the first restaurants to celebrate Maltese cuisine and it is probably still the best. The specials board will guide you as to the freshest fare, although their *casatella siciliana* dessert is a must-try.

Sciacca Grill

South Street; tel: 2123 7222; www. sciaccamalta.com; daily noon–3.30pm and 6–10.30pm; €€€

It's all about the meat here at the capital's new grill house. You'll choose your cut from a deli-style counter and it will be cooked to perfection. Do leave room for dessert too.

Trabuxu Bistro

8/9 South Street; tel: 2122 0357; www. trabuxu.com.mt/bistro; Mon–Sat noon–3pm, 7–11pm; €€

The sister restaurant to the popular Trabuxu Winebar, it is run by a delightful husband-and-wife team who have created a fantastic fusion menu that looks as good as it tastes. Book well ahead.

Zero Sei

75 Old Theatre Street; tel: 2122 2010; www.zeroseimalta.com; Tue–Sun noon–2.30pm and 7–11pm; €€

Situated right opposite the Manoel Theatre, this Italian eatery is the perfect pre- or post-dinner spot. The owner is Roman, as is the food. The pasta is some of the best anywhere on the island.

The Blue Elephant is your best bet for authentic Thai food

St Julian's

The Avenue

Gort Street; tel: 2135 1753; www.
theavenuemalta.com; daily noon–2.30pm
and 6–11.30pm; €

This is one for the families: a lively restaurant with an extensive menu that
will please all ages and tastes. From
pizza and pasta to fish and grills, it
offers just about everything you can
imagine.

Barracuda

194 Main Street; tel: 2133 1817; www.
barracudarestaurant.com; daily 6.30–
10.30pm; €€€€

Considered one of the very best restaurants on the island, this is the ideal
location for a special occasion. Enjoy
delicious meat, fish and shellfish dishes
along with magnificent views of the bay.

Blue Elephant

Hilton Malta, Portomaso; tel: 2138 3383;
www.blueelephant.com/malta; daily
6.30–10.30pm; €€€

Arguably the best Thai restaurant on
the island, the hospitality, setting and
cuisine is flawless. The tasting menu is
highly recommended.

Caviar & Bull

Marina Hotel Corinthia Beach Resort, St
George's Bay: tel: 2759 3301; https://
caviarandbull.com/malta; daily 6.30–11pm,
Sun noon–3.30pm; €€€

Run by local celebrity chef Marvin
Gauci, who is also the chef patron of
Tarragon in St Paul's Bay, Caviar &
Bull combines molecular gastronomy
with fantastic Mediterranean flavours.
We recommend the cocktails too.

Hard Rock Café

Level 2, Baystreet Shopping Complex,
St George's Bay; tel: 2138 0983; www.
hardrock.com/cafes/malta; daily 11.30am–
11pm; €€

Expect American favourites, including
their legendary burgers, served in a
lively atmosphere and typical Hard Rock
décor. Their two-for-one Happy Hour is
at 6pm Mon–Fri.

I Monelli

63A Wilga Street; tel: 2136 0036; Wed–Mon
noon–2.45pm, 7–11.45pm; €€

Come here for an authentic Sicilian
culinary experience. The antipasti,
which you can choose at the counter,
is fresh and delicious, while the pizzas
are known to be some of the best on
the island, all baked in a wood-fired
oven.

Shiva's

Dragonara Road Paceville; tel: 2138
4399; www.shivasindiancuisine.com;
Wed–Mon 6.30–11pm, Sun noon–4pm
also; €€

Arguably the best Indian restaurant in
the area, Shiva's goes right to the heart
of Indian cooking traditions. There's
lots for vegetarians to enjoy here,
although meat lovers will also be well
taken care of.

Fried Pasta (Tarja Moqlija), a local speciality

Waterbiscuit

St George's Bay, InterContinental Malta; tel: 2376 2225; www.malta.intercontinental. com; daily 12.30–11.30pm; €€€

Refined and elegant, this restaurant doubles as a wine and cocktail bar. The menu never disappoints, and it is nice to see it being prepared in the open kitchen.

Zeri's

Portomaso; tel: 2135 9559; www. zerisrestaurant.com; daily 7–11pm; €€€

Locals know that Zeri's, under the firm guidance of chef patron Mark Zerafa, never fails to disappoint. Anything with lobster in it will be delicious, as is the Angus fillet, always cooked to perfection.

Zest

25 St George's Road, Spinola Bay; tel: 2138 7600; www.zestflavours.com; Mon–Sat 7–11pm; €€€

Combining the very best from the East and West, Zest is stylish and enticing. The menu combines dishes from Thailand, Indonesia and Japan as well as from all over Europe, so you can start with tepanyaki and finish with crème brûlée.

Sliema & Gzira

4 Amici

81 The Strand, Gzira; tel: 2133 0755; Wed–Mon noon–2.45pm, 7–10.45pm; €€

This is probably the best restaurant on the Gzira promenade. You'll find an innovative menu that offers predominantly Sicilian cuisine always prepared with the best of what's in season.

The Chophouse

Tigné Point; tel: 2060 3355; www. chophouse.com.mt; daily 7–11pm; €€€

From the finest whiskies to the very best cuts of meat, the Chophouse is the perfect place for a good night out. The views across to Valletta are also stunning.

hiMù

195 The Strand; Gzira; tel: 2788 0400; daily 9am–midnight; €€

If you've never been to a mozzarella bar, then this is your chance. Run by an Italian team, you'll be able to try mozzarella varieties from across Italy, in salads or sandwiches, or to take away.

La Cuccagna

47 Amery Street; tel: 2134 6703; www. cuccagnamalta.com; Tue–Sun 7–11.30pm; €€

Renowned for its pizzas, Cuccagna is laid back and family-run. If you don't fancy pizza, then the salads, oven-baked ribs and gluten-free options are also tasty.

Mint

30-39 Luzio Junction, Stella Maris Street; tel: 2133 7177; www.mintmalta.com; Mon–Fri 8am–4pm; €

This gourmet café just off the seafront serves sweet and savoury specials

Presentation is of the essence at De Mondion

including vegan lasagne, delicious salads and pies. Their cakes are made fresh and go down beautifully with one of their fresh juices. A good, healthy choice.

New York Best
Qui-Si-Sana seafront; tel: 2728 2899; www.newyorkbest.com; daily 9am–11pm; €

This local chain of gourmet burgers has really taken off and locals love the authentic American fare. The burgers are the highlight here, but there's also sourdough pizza, hot dogs and milkshakes to tempt you.

Piccolo Padre
194/195 Main Street; tel: 2134 4875; www.piccolopadre.com; daily 6.15–10.30pm, Sun noon–3pm also; €€

Pizza is the order of the day at this family-run establishment, which has gorgeous views out over Balluta Bay. Try to secure one of their balcony tables if you can, and do leave room for their homemade desserts.

Ta' Xbiex Waterpolo Club
Ta' Xbiex Sea Front; tel: 2733 0144; www.taxbiexwaterpoloclub.com; daily noon–3pm, Mon–Sat 7–10.30pm also; €€€

The menu here is as good as its fantastic views over Valletta. The selection includes pizza, pasta, grilled meats and fresh fish, as well as their popular chocolate fondant dessert.

Vecchia Napoli
255 Tower Road; tel: 2134 3434; www.vecchianapoli.com; daily noon–4pm and 6–10.30pm; €

Long established as one of the best pizza places on the island, you can dine indoors or out at this relaxed Italian eatery. While pizza is their speciality, the pasta and grills are also very good.

Mdina, Rabat & Attard

Bacchus
1 Inguanez Street, Mdina; tel: 2145 4981; www.bacchus.com.mt; daily 10.30am–10.30pm; €€

The French-inspired cuisine at this Mdina stalwart is absolutely delicious and always impressive. The food blends home-cooking with inimitable French flair.

De Mondion
The Xara Palace Relais & Châteaux, Council Square, Mdina; tel: 2145 0560; www.demondion.com; daily 7.30–10.30pm; €€€€

Rated among the top restaurants on the island, this fine dining establishment is located on the top floor of the luxurious Xara Palace Hotel (see page 91). The tasting menu will suit a very special occasion, especially when paired with their suggested wines.

Fontanella Tea Garden
1 Bastion Square, Mdina; tel: 2145 4264; www.fontanellateagarden.com; daily

Café Del Mar, the perfect place to enjoy sunset in style

10am–11.30pm; €€
You can literally sit on the bastions of this popular café – that is, if you get a table. It is busy but fast moving. People flock here for the delicious cakes, especially their strawberry meringue. The perfect place for afternoon tea.

Rickshaw

Corinthia Palace Hotel & Spa, De Paule Avenue, Attard; tel: 2544 2190; www.corinthia.com/palace; Tue–Sat 7–11pm; €€€
This is one of the best pan-Asian restaurants on the island, combining dishes from Malaysia, Thailand, Indonesia and the Philippines. The daily specials are always a good choice.

Villa Corinthia

Corinthia Palace Hotel & Spa, De Paule Avenue, Attard; tel: 2144 0301; www.corinthia.com/palace; daily 7–10pm; €€€
Set in the same hotel as Rickshaw, above, this fine-dining establishment is run by Stefan Hogan, one of Malta's most celebrated chefs. The eclectic menu features fish, meat and pasta dishes. The villa makes for a luxurious setting for afternoon tea.

Yue Bistro by Munchies

Labour Avenue, Naxxar; tel: 2258 9888; www.yuemalta.com/yue-bistro; daily 9am–11pm; €
Laid back, with a tasty menu of snacks and some heartier dishes, this is an excellent pit stop just down the road from the centre of Naxxar. The focus is on healthy cooking, although the desserts are quite decadent.

Bugibba, Qawra and Mellieha

The Arches

113 Gorg Borg Olivier Street, Mellieha; tel: 2152 3460; www.thearchesmalta.com; Tue–Sat 6.30–11pm; €€€
This was among Malta's first fine-dining restaurants, and many think it is still the best. Start with a drink in the lounge, and then head through to the elegant dining room to enjoy the innovative Mediterranean menu.

Bouquet Garni

4 Gorg Borg Olivier Street, Mellieha; tel: 2152 2234; Mon–Sat 6.30–10.30pm; €€€
Consistently rated among the very best restaurants in the north of Malta, you'd be hard-pressed to find a better fish menu. That said, meat lovers won't be disappointed – and the desserts are worth waiting for, too.

Café Del Mar

Trunciera Street, Qawra; tel: 2258 8144; www.cafedelmar.com.mt; daily 10am–11pm, Sat–Sun until midnight; €€
This is a summer hot spot in Malta, attracting a glamourous crowd to eat, drink and then dance the night away. There's a relaxed menu at the Lido through the day, as well as speciality choices for lunch and dinner.

Enjoy views of Golden Bay from Essence

Commando Restaurant

Iz-Zjara tal-Papa Gwanni Pawlu II-26 ta' Mejju 1990 Square, Mellieha; tel: 9949 8843; www.commandorestaurant.com; Tue–Sat 6.30–10pm, Sun noon–3pm; €€
This restaurant and wine bar is perched on a hill with beautiful views. This is a good choice for authentic, local dishes, including the perfectly cooked rabbit, followed by their pastries and desserts.

Essence

Radisson Blu Resort & Spa, Malta Golden Sands, Mellieha; tel: 2356 1000; Tue–Sat 6.30–11pm; €€€
This unique dining venue, with a five-star service, stands out from the crowd – helped by the beautiful views of Golden Bay. The bar here is also lovely for a pre-dinner cocktail.

Gozo & Comino

Arzella

Ghar Qawqla Street, Marsalforn; tel: 2155 4662; www.ristorantearzella.com; Wed–Mon 11am–3pm and 6–10pm; €€
A good choice along the bay in Marsalforn, and easily overlooked. The food is consistent and the view absolutely beautiful. Their trademark fish platter is especially good.

Beppe's

il-Minqa, Marsalforn; tel: 2750 0567; Thu–Tue 6.30–10pm; €€
The team here prides itself on only serving up the freshest, seasonal fare, and the results are delicious. The menu is experimental but despite this the prices are very reasonable.

D-Bar

St Joseph Square, Qala; tel: 2155 6242; www.gozo.com/dbar; Tue–Sun 6–11pm, Sat–Sun 11.30am–2pm also; €€
This family friendly bar and restaurant specialises in local dishes. Expect large portions of everything, including the excellent pizzas. The family's old black-and-white photos add a personal touch.

Ic-Cima

St Simon Street, Xlendi; tel: 2155 8407; www.cimarestaurant.com; Wed–Mon noon–2.30pm, 6.30–10.30pm; €€
This rooftop restaurant has wonderful views of the bay below. The menu is mostly Mediterranean, with excellent pasta, fish and meat, and a small menu dedicated solely to Gozitan dishes.

Il-Panzier

39 Charity Street, Rabat; tel: 2155 9979; daily noon–2.30pm, 6.30–9pm; €€
Well located in the heart of the capital, Il-Panzier is a garden restaurant with a lovely atmosphere. Run by a Sicilian family, the food is true to that region but makes the most of the freshest Gozitan produce.

Latini

Il-Menqa, Marsalforn; tel: 2155 0950;

The vaulted interior of Ta' Frenc

www.latinirestaurant.com; Wed–Mon 9am–2pm, 6–9.30pm; €€
This is the spot for good Mediterranean fare in a family friendly atmosphere. Seafood reigns supreme here, and we recommend the specials from the chef's menu, as it changes regularly to make the most of seasonal produce.

Patrick's Lounge & Restaurant
Europe Street, Rabat; tel: 2156 6667; www.patrickstmun.com; Tue–Sat 7–9.30pm; €€€
Award-winning Patrick's is a local favourite, and Maltese will make the trip to Gozo especially to enjoy a meal here. Start with a drink in the chic lounge while you peruse the menu, then enjoy your meal in the elegant dining room. Leave room for dessert.

Rew Rew
Mgarr ix-Xini; tel: 7985 4007; daily 10am–4pm; €€€
Located in the secluded bay that played the backdrop to Angelina Jolie's *By the Sea* (2015), Rew Rew is a fish place like no other. While the setting is simple the food isn't cheap, but it is delicious.

Sicilia Bella
Manuel de Vilhena Street, Mgarr; tel: 2156 3588; Tue–Sat 7–10pm; €€
This was one of the first proper Sicilian eateries to open on the Maltese Islands, and it has kept its solid rep-

utation. The shellfish here is always reliable, and the spaghetti with clams is a true favourite.

Ta' Frenc
Ghajn Damma Street, Xaghra; tel: 2155 3888; www.tafrencrestaurant.com; Wed–Mon noon–1.30pm and 7–9.30pm; €€€
This restaurant promises local fine dining at its very best, and the team of chefs never disappoints. Many of the ingredients are grown in the gardens here, making them as fresh as can be. A good selection of meat, fish and vegetarian dishes are served.

Ta' Pennellu
Marina Street, Marsalforn; tel: 2155 9730; www.pennellu.com; Wed–Mon 10am–2pm, 6.30–10.30pm; €€€
One of the best restaurants in the charming bay of Marsalforn, Ta' Pennellu is located right by the sea. Child friendly, there is something for everyone, including a wonderful selection of freshly-caught fish.

Ta' Vestru
5 St Joseph Square, Qala: tel: 2155 9090; Tue–Sun 11am–2pm, 6–11.30pm; €€
Located in a traditional Gozitan townhouse, the menu here matches its authentic setting, with delicious pizza, stewed rabbit, fresh fish and other Gozitan specialities. A pleasant and relaxed dining experience.

Bright lights at the Manoel Theatre

NIGHTLIFE

Nightlife in Malta is as varied as they come, with an eclectic mix of theatres showing everything from modern comedies to Shakespearean plays – mostly in English – to bars with live music, clubs open till the small hours of the morning, and an arts cinema showing the latest blockbusters as well as live plays and operas from all over Europe.

Valletta

Theatre, dance, opera, art
Blitz
St Lucia Street; tel: 2122 4992; www.thisisblitz.com
Founded and run by local artist Alexandra Pace, Blitz is Malta's only independent, contemporary art space. Throughout the year, it holds numerous art exhibitions by various painters, photographers and sculptors. Seasonal networking events for creatives are held here, with the dates and information for tickets published on Facebook a few weeks before the event. The information will be listed under an event called 'Hey Disco'.

Manoel Theatre
Old Theatre Street; tel: 2124 6389; www.teatrumanoel.com.mt; guided tours Mon–Fri 9.30am–4.30pm, Sat 9.30am–12.30pm

Established by Grand Master de Vilhena of the Knights of St John, the Manoel is one of the world's oldest working theatres. Set aside the numerous plays, operas and dance shows produced here, the theatre is an architectural gem in its own right, with its 400-year-old acoustical technology that still allows performances to forgo the use of microphones. The Baroque Music Festival also takes place here.

Mediterranean Conference Centre
Triq L-isptar; tel: 2124 3840; www.mcc.com.mt
This 16th-century building was the official hospital of the Knights of St John, and is still well-known by its original name, the Sacra Infermeria. Today, it is a venue used for conferences and fairs, including the National Book Festival in November, as well as dance, theatre and concert productions.

St James Cavalier Centre for Creativity
Castille Place; tel: 2122 3200; www.sjcav.org
Incorporating an art gallery, an arts cinema and a theatre, St James Cavalier was a present to the nation for the new millennium. It has now become

one of Malta's best-loved and best-known culture venues. Theatre performances are scheduled throughout the year, but particularly between October and May. There are also regular exhibitions, film screenings as well as live streaming of foreign opera, ballets and theatre productions.

Nightlife
Charles Grech Café & Cocktail Bar
10, Republic Street; tel: 2122 8848; www. charlesgrech.com
This upmarket café, bar and liqueur and cigar store hybrid is the in-place in Valletta right now. Office workers get their morning coffee here, and come back again in the evening for an *aperitivo*, served with appetisers. Go in the early evening to secure a table on Republic Street, the perfect place for people-watching.

Gugar – Hangout & Bar
89A, Republic Street; tel: 2703 2837
Started by a group of friends just a few years ago, Gugar has quickly become one of Valletta's most popular bars serving an eclectic and somewhat eccentric clientele. The bar is particularly renowned for its vegetarian and vegan food; and when you visit don't be surprised if there is a filigree workshop or tropical party going on.

Legligin Wine Bar
St Lucia Street; tel: 2122 1699

The word 'legligin' comes from the Maltese verb 'tlegleg', which translates to 'guzzle' True to its name, this is the perfect bar for a night out drinking wine with friends, and is the haunt of theatre actors and local socialites. The place is incredibly small, however, so go early to get a good spot.

StrEat Whisky & Bistro
Strait Street; tel: 7778 7328
Although it's only been open since 2012, StrEat has become one of Malta's most popular bars, especially popular with office workers for *aperitivo*. Regular whisky tasting events are held, and a mixed menu serving everything from pasta to steak is offered.

Tico Tico
61 Strait Street; tel: 2122 0449
Reminiscent of Strait Street's heyday back when British and American sailors roamed the street in search of fun, Tico Tico is slowly becoming a nightlife institution. Drinks here are relatively cheap and the crowd always jubilant. Friday and Saturday nights tend to be the best times to visit.

St Julian's

Nightlife
Club Havana
Triq San Gorg; tel: 2137 4500
Located in the heart of the party-mile within St Julian's, Club Havana has

The night is young at Havana

become the hub of Malta's night-life scene. Thousands descend onto its dance floor on Friday and Saturday nights – and Sundays, Mondays and Wednesdays in the summer – to dance to the hippest tunes and to drink till the early hours of the morning. ID is required at the door.

Havana808Club

85 St.Georges Road; tel: 2137 4500

Located below Club Havana, Havana808Club has quickly become one of Malta's coolest clubs, attracting Malta's fashion elite, models, bloggers and fashion photographers. Wednesdays are the best day to visit in the summer, while Fridays remain the favourite in winter. Prices are reasonable, so expect to see many guzzling champagne in the VIP area.

Level 22

Hilton Business Tower; tel: 2310 2222; www.22.com.mt

Located on the 22nd level of the Hilton Business Tower, Level 22 is one of Malta's chicest venues and thus often hosts exclusive events. The views, which extend to half-way across the island, matched by the ultra-modern décor, attract Malta's bold and beautiful. The bar team are particularly renowned for their cocktails.

Michaelangelo Club Lounge

Qube Level 1, St Rita Steps; tel: 7977 2017

As Malta's only gay club, Michaelangelo Club Lounge attracts an eclectic crowd as everyone is welcome here. The music is good and the drinks are generally cheap too, with DJs pumping tunes till closing time on weekends.

Casinos

Dragonara Casino

Dragonara Palace, Dragonara Road; tel: 2138 2362; www.dragonaracasino.com

Open 24 hours a day, the Dragonara Casino is housed within an 1870 property built for a Maltese marquis. First opened in 1964, it has since had a €14 million-euro refurbishment and now boasts state-of-the-art gaming equipment. ID is required at the door; foreigners must be at least 18 years of age, locals 25; admission after 11pm incurs a charge. Dress appropriately.

Portomaso Casino

Portomaso; tel: 2138 3777; www.portomasocasino.com

The swanky casino, located in one of Malta's most exclusive postcodes, has all the casino classics. Texas Hold 'Em poker tournaments and cash games are held daily. The dress code is strict – no shorts or sleeveless shirts allowed – so dress smart casual. Transport is available on request; alternatively if you have a car, you can take advantage of the free parking. ID is required at the door; foreigners must be at least 18 years of age, locals 25.

Otello opera at Teatru Astra

Sliema

Nightlife
Black Gold
93-95, The Strand; tel: 2133 4808
Located in one of the most desirable spots on the island, Black Gold is a favourite among the 'in' crowd, with many foreigners descending here after a day at the beach in the summer months. Football games are often shown on the big screens. In the late evenings, this place becomes a proper club, with live bands on Thursdays, Fridays and Saturdays.

Hamrun

Theatre
Blue Box
Mspace, Triq Oscar Zammit; tel: 2124 6619; www.masquerademalta.com
Run by one of Malta's most influential families in theatre, Blue Box is the only establishment in the area solely dedicated to theatrical productions. And thanks to a string of successful and sell-out shows, it is fast becoming one of the island's most diverse spaces, with productions ranging from drama to comedy and musicals. Visit their website for a full list of upcoming productions.

Gozo

Theatre, dance, opera, art
Teatru Astra
9 Republic Street; tel: 2155 0985; www.

teatruastra.org.mt
Teatru Astra is one of Malta's major theatres; local and international opera singers have performed here, including Maltese tenor Joseph Calleja. An opera is scheduled in October, with the Festival Mediterranea taking place over the last few months of the year. Tickets for opera cost between €50–70.

Teatru Aurora
Republic Street; tel: 2156 2974; www. teatruaurora.com
Located opposite the Astra, the Aurora is another famed theatre. Their yearly opera, also taking place in October, is a sell out every year, and tickets to the performance should be booked as early as possible to avoid disappointment. Their cultural calendar also features ballets, dramas and concerts. Tickets to their events cost between €5–80.

Nightlife
La Grotta
Xlendi; tel: 2155 1149
The biggest club in Malta with big names like David Guetta, DJ Molella, Ritchie Hawtin (Plastikman), Mr C (The Shamen) and Alex Gaudino all having played here. La Grotta is one of Malta's most popular outdoor clubs, perfectly situated overlooking Xlendi Bay. In winter, the indoor part of the venue, the café lounge, is just as popular. Admission costs between €7–10.

Boat trips are a highlight of any visit to the islands

A–Z

A

Addresses

Addresses in Malta are similar to those all around Europe, with home number, street name, locality and postcode in that particular order. A little glossary is useful though: *'Sqaq'* means 'alley'; *'strada'* and *'triq'* mean 'street'; *'trejqa'* means 'little street'; *'trejqet'* means 'street of'; and *'vjal'* means 'avenue'.

Age restrictions

According to Maltese law, persons under 17 are not allowed to drink alcohol. The minimum age for driving with a valid licence is 18, but for renting a car, in most cases, a driver must be 21 or over. It is unlawful to sell or give tobacco products to persons under 16 years of age, and to smoke or make use of tobacco products before the age of 18. The legal age of consent in Malta is also 18.

B

Budgeting

Mid-range hotels charge around €100–150 a night for a double room, including breakfast. Lower on that spectrum you can expect to pay anywhere between €40–80 for a double room, while expensive hotels can cost upwards of €300 a night for a double room. A three-course dinner for two in a mid-range restaurant, including a bottle of wine and water, will set you back around €70; lunch for two at a café, including water, will cost around €30. Wine by the glass, in restaurants, is normally priced at around €4 while a beer will cost you €3 on average. Fuel is more expensive than in most European countries, and public transport remains the cheapest mode of transportation. Get a Tallinja card explore (see page 118) to avoid paying up to €3 per single journey. EU citizens under 18 and over 65 are allowed free entry to main sights, and students get concessions.

C

Children

Children are always made to feel welcome, and restaurants often have a kids' menu or will happily prepare a simple pasta with cheese or tomato sauce for your little ones. At the beach, children usually wear bathing suits and it is not customary to let them run around naked. Babysitting services are available in many of the upper-range hotels. Children under the age of six are usually admitted to sights free of charge and those from six to 16 at a reduced price.

Gozo's colourful glassware

Clothing

The customs here are the same as other southern European countries and cities. Not wearing a shirt in public is frowned upon, and men may be stopped by the police and asked to put their T-shirt back on. Sunbathing topless in public is illegal for women.

If you're visiting Malta in the summer, cotton clothes are recommended, along with shorts and flip-flops. Be aware that, to enter churches, your shoulders must be covered and that shorts cannot go above the knee. If you're visiting the island in winter, pack a waterproof jacket and shoes. Layering T-shirts, cardigans and jackets is advisable.

Crime and safety

While Malta is considered one of the safest countries in the world, petty crime rate is on the increase, so general precautions are advisable, such as not leaving your valuables unattended or on display. Reassuringly, Malta has some of the lowest figures for more serious crime.

Customs

Free exchange of non-duty-free goods for personal use is allowed between EU countries. For non-EU citizens the duty-free allowances are 200 cigarettes, 50 cigars, 1 litre of spirits, 2 litres of wine and 16 litres of beer. If you plan to enter or leave Malta with €10,000 or more in cash (or its equivalent in other curren-cies), you must declare it to the customs authorities.

Live animals fall under the responsibility of the Veterinary Regulation Directorate within the Agriculture & Fisheries Regulation Department of the Ministry for Sustainable Development, the Environment and Climate Change.

To contact Customs at the Malta International Airport, you can call +356 21248 044/9868 from 8am–5pm CET, or by sending an e-mail to mia.customs@gov.mt.

D

Disabled travellers

Most sites and attractions, as well as churches and government buildings, have disabled access; yet getting round may prove quite difficult. There are narrow pavements and streets without pavements to negociate, and it gets even more difficult when decorations are up for the village *festas* in the summer months.

Beach Trotters for wheelchair users can be found at Ghadira Bay, Golden Bay and St George's Bay. Contact the beach supervisor on site at the respective beach (mid-June to mid-September, daily 10am–6pm).

For more information contact the National Commission Persons with Disability (KNPD), before you travel (Bugeja Institute, Braille Street, Santa Venera, SVR 1619; tel: 2278 8555; helpdesk@knpd.org; www.knpd.org).

Colourful Pride parade in Valletta

E

Electricity

Malta's electrical supply is 230 volts, 50 hertz. The three-pin, rectangular plug system is used – similar to the one in the UK. Adapters are needed for most countries, and these can be bought from numerous stores around the island.

Embassies and consulates

If your passport is lost or stolen, you will need to obtain a police report and have proof of identity to get a new one. For consulates and embassies in Malta, see below:

Australian Embassy: Ta' Xbiex Terrace, Ta' Xbiex; tel: 2133 8201; https://malta.embassy.gov.au.

Canadian Consulate: Demajo House, 103 Archbishop Street, Valletta, VLT 09; tel: 2552 3233; www.canadainternational.gc.ca; note that the Consulate in Valletta offers only emergency assistance, not the normal list of consular services.

Irish Embassy: Whitehall Mansions, Ta' Xbiex Seafront, Ta' Xbiex, XBX 1026; tel: 2133 4744; www.dfa.ie/irish-embassy/malta.

UK Embassy: Whitehall Mansions, Ta' Xbiex Seafront, Ta' Xbiex; tel: 2323 0000; www.gov.uk/government/world/malta.

US Embassy: Ta' Qali National Park, Attard, ATD 4000; tel: 2561 4196; http://mt.usembassy.gov.

Emergencies

General emergences: 112; Police: 2122 4001; Fire: 112; Ambulance: 112; Breakdown/ road assistance: 2124 2222/2144 2422 (Malta), 2155 8844 (Gozo).

Etiquette

As aforementioned, wearing short skirts or shorts and sleeveless tops in churches is frowned upon and may even cause offence. Casual clothes are quite acceptable in most restaurants, yet swimwear should be avoided. If invited for dinner by locals, you are expected to always bring something: pastries, wine or flowers are always appreciated.

H

Health

Inoculations

No vaccinations are required to enter Malta.

Health care and insurance

All EU countries have reciprocal arrangements for medical services, and UK residents should obtain a European Health Insurance Card through www.nhs.uk.

Australian nationals are also entitled to receive help with the cost of essential medical treatment in Malta. To be eligible a person must present his or her Australian passport, or another valid passport, which shows he or she is a permanent resident in Australia, as

Traditional boats, or luzzus, are still very much in use

well as a valid Medicare card. To obtain a Medicare card, please visit a service centre. Medicine is not usually subsidised under the Reciprocal Health Care Agreement, and this does not replace private travel insurance.

Both of the above only cover medical care, not emergency repatriation costs or additional expenses. It is therefore advisable, and for non-EU residents essential, to have travel insurance to cover all eventualities.

Pharmacies and hospitals

A pharmacy is identified by a green cross, and these can be found in every town and village on the islands. Most pharmacies open during normal working hours, with the pharmacy at the Malta International Airport open till 10pm. On Sundays and public holidays, pharmacies work on a roster; this roster is available at http://health.gov.mt/en/PharmacyRoster.

Malta also has three 24-hour health centres: one in Mosta (Constitution Street; tel: 2141 1065), Paola (Pjazza A. De Paule; tel: 2169 1314) and Floriana (F.S. Fenech Street; tel: 2124 3314).

The main hospital is Mater Dei Hospital on Triq Dun Karm, L-Imsida (tel: 2545 0000).

I

Internet facilities

While there aren't many Internet cafés in Malta, most cafés, restaurants and bars now offer free Wi-Fi to their customers (there will usually be a sign on the door). Should the service be password protected, ask a member of staff for details.

L

Language

Both Maltese and English are the official languages of the Maltese Islands; with English spoken widely and well across the islands. Italian is also spoken by a large sector of Maltese nationals. See page 118 for a selection of useful phrases.

LGBTQ travellers

Malta has recently seen great advancements in LGBT rights, with civil unions, adoptions by gay couples, a transgender act, and gender-neutral terminology acts all passed by Parliament in recent years. Even so, displaying affection in public may still receive negative comments.

Malta's only gay club is Michaelangelo Club Lounge (http://at-michelangelo.com), located on Santa Rita Steps in St Julian's. Admission fees are sometimes charged. The club is open until 4am on Friday and Saturday. Monaliza Bar & Lounge on Triq L-Assedju Il-Kbir in Valletta has a mixed gay and straight crowd. Every year, a number of gay parties are organised.

For more information consult MGRM (the Malta Gay Rights Movements) website, www.maltagayrights.org.

M

Media

Newspapers

Most print media in Malta is in English. The three, leading newspapers in English are *The Times of Malta* (daily), *The Malta Independent* (daily) and *MaltaToday* (Wednesdays and Sundays). On Sundays, these newspapers come with a myriad of magazine supplements including those about lifestyle, arts and culture, property and food. Malta does not have any printed listing magazines, but www.visitmalta.com has a What's On section.

Radio

Radio is still widely listened to in Malta, with 89.7 Bay (www.bay.com.mt) and XFM 100.2 FM (www.xfm.com.mt) both running various shows in English, including the news.

Television

TV shows and programmes are mostly in Maltese, with very few English-speaking shows. However ONE TV (www.one.com.mt) runs weekly shows in English.

Money

Currency

The currency in Malta is the euro (€). A euro is divided into 100 cents with 5, 20 and 50-cent coins, and 1 and 2 euro coins. The euro notes are 5, 10, 20, 50, 100, 200 and 500 (which is still in circulation but no longer printed).

Credit cards

Except in smaller villages, major credit cards are accepted by shops, hotels, restaurants and petrol stations. It is advisable to always keep some cash on hand, particularly when visiting markets.

Cash machines

ATMs are found all over the island, even in small towns. Instructions are given in English, French and other languages. They are the easiest and generally the cheapest way to obtain cash. ATM machines at hotels are not common.

Taxes

Malta imposes an 18 percent Value Added Tax (VAT) on most goods and services, with VAT on accommodation being 7 percent. Non-EU citizens are entitled to a refund of around 12 percent if they spend over €175 at stores in Malta. You will need to keep all receipts and present them at the designated office at the Malta International Airport (if you're leaving by plane) or the Valletta Waterfront (if you're leaving by boat). A tax of €0.50 per bed-night, capped at €5, for adults (over 18s) is applicable.

Tipping

Service charges are rarely included

Festa in Sliema

in restaurant bills, and a tip is often expected. This should be between 10–15 percent of the total bill, although this is not a must. Tipping the staff at a bar, hairdressers, masseurs, taxi drivers etc. is not expected but welcomed.

Opening hours

Typical working hours in Malta are 9am to 5pm, with shops opening from 9/10am till 7pm; some newsagents and grocers open as early as 6am. Shops in Valletta, as well as in Sliema and St Julian's do not close in the afternoons, but most shops in the various villages close between noon/1pm–3/4pm. Saturday morning is normally business as usual, with some not reopening after lunch. The majority of shops – apart from a handful in Sliema and St Julian's – are closed on Sundays. Most shops in Valletta, Sliema and St Julian's also open on public holidays, excluding Good Friday, Christmas Day and New Year's Day.

P

Post

The national postal system in Malta is run by Malta Post (www.maltapost. com), and is considered to be efficient. A stamp for a standard letter or postcard to European countries costs around €0.50 and €0.70 to the US. Stamps can be purchased from Post Offices located all over the island, including the two in Valletta, one at Dar Annona, Misrah Kastilja, and the other on Triq L-Ifran. Most stationaries and souvenir shops also stock stamps.

Public holidays

New Year's Day 1 January
St Paul's Day 10 February
St Joseph's Day 19 March
Freedom Day 31 March
Good Friday Variable
Workers' Day 1 May
'Sette Giugno' 7 June
St Peter and St Paul (*L-Imnarja*) 29 June
Feast of the Assumption 15 August
Feast of Our Lady of Victories Day 8 September
Independence Day 21 September
Feast of the Immaculate Conception 8 December
Republic Day 13 December
Christmas Day 25 December

R

Religion

Malta's official religion is Roman Catholicism; yet the State is tolerant of all other religions. Religious tolerance is practiced throughout the country, too. Muslim, Buddhist, Protestant, and Jewish communities, among others, can be found on the island, with

British phone boxes can still be seen in Valletta

an Anglican Cathedral situated in Valletta and a Mosque in Paola.

S

Smoking

Smoking is widely accepted in Malta, but it is illegal to smoke inside commercial buildings, including bars, clubs and restaurants. Most places have smoking areas or have ashtrays clearly displayed outside their main doors. Smoking in playing fields is also illegal, but it is acceptable in other outdoor public spaces.

T

Telephones

For calls within Malta from an international number, telephone numbers must be preceded by (00)356. Malta and Gozo share the same country code, and there are no city or area codes used here.

International dialing codes are (44) for the UK, (353) for Ireland, (61) for Australia and (1) for US and Canada.

Public telephone boxes are available all over the island, yet most have fallen into disrepair.

Mobile (Cell) phones

Malta has a number of mobile service providers, with GO, Vodafone and Melita being the three most renowned. SIM cards can be purchased from one of their shops located all around the island and typically cost €10. Operating frequency bands in Malta are 2G, 3G and 4G.

Time zones

The Maltese Islands follow the Central European Time (GMT+1) but, from the last Sunday in March to the last Sunday in October, the clocks advance one additional hour to become GMT+2. This means in summer, when it is noon in Malta, it will be 11am in London and 6am in New York.

Toilets

Toilets in Malta are similar to those used all over the Western world. When out and about, public toilets can be

Sunset over Valletta

Splash & Fun park

und in various localities around the land, and you can also use toilets in afés, bars and shopping complexes. uying a drink when using an establishment's facilities will be appreciated, although not necessary. Major tes and museums should also have easonable facilities.

ourist information

ne staff at all Tourist Information ffices is fluent in English and, most f the time, at least one other language, most probably Italian, French, erman or Spanish. These offices can e found at most tourist hotspots, and re open every day including Sundays nd public holidays, except on Christmas Day, New Year's Day, Good Friday nd Easter Sunday. A local, freephone ervice is available by calling on 8007 230.

alletta, 229, Merchants Street; tel: 122 0193

alletta Waterfront, Pinto Wharf; tel: 122 0633

Malta International Airport, Arrivals ounge; tel: 2369 6073/4

Birgu, Xatt is-Sajjieda; tel: 2180 0145

Mdina, Torre dello Standardo, St Publius Square; tel: 2145 4480

Mellieha, Misrah Iz-Zjara tal-Papa Gwanni Pawlu II; tel: 2152 4666

Sliema, Plaza Commercial Centre; tel: 2136 3691 (closed on Sundays)

St Paul's Bay, Misrah il-Bajja; tel: 2141 9176

Victoria, Gozo, No. 17, Independence Square; tel: 2291 5452

Tours and guides

There are various companies in Malta that offer a unique way of experiencing the island.

Captain Morgan Cruises (www. captainmorgan.com.mt) offer a variety of on-sea tours of the Maltese islands, including a Harbour Cruise, a Comino & the Blue Lagoon Cruise, the Underwater Safari and the Romantic Evening Harbour Cruise. They also specialise in Jeep Safaris and the Land Rover Defender Tours.

Malta Sightseeing (www.mal tasightseeing.com) offer a Vintage Bus Tour to the Three Cities (Vittoriosa, Cospicua and Senglea) on one of the first two wooden-clad buses purchased in 1921 by the Cottonera Motor Bus Company.

Malta Shore Excursions (www. maltashoreexcursions.com) offer historical, cultural, scenic, fun and adventure tours, as well as tours of Comino and Gozo to those visiting Malta while on a cruise.

Transport

Arriving by air

Malta currently has one airport, the Malta International Airport (www.mal tairport.com). This caters for all three inhabited islands, and those staying in Gozo or Comino will need to land here, get a taxi or bus to Cirkewwa in

the north and ferry it to Mgarr in Gozo.

Located in Luqa, the airport is 16 minutes away by car from Valletta, 19 minutes from Sliema, 18 minutes from St Julian's, about 45 minutes from Cirkewwa, and 12 minutes to Marsaxlokk.

The local bus system is run by Malta Public Transport (www.publictrans port.com.mt), with four express routes (X1, X2, X3, X4) to various localities from the airport. The service runs daily between (approximately) 5am till 11pm. Buses are almost never punctual and traffic jams are frequent, so make sure you give yourself plenty of time to get to your destination.

Arriving by rail

Malta has no rail service, and it is not connected to mainland Europe in any way. You can, however, travel to Sicily and get a ferry from Catania and Pozzallo to Valletta.

The Italian mainland is linked to Sicily by train, with Milan, Rome and Naples being the best connecting stations to the south. Unfortunately, the great improvements in the Italian rail system do not extend to Sicily, and the overnight sleeper service from Sicily to northern Italy has been cancelled.

There is a daily service between Rome and Palermo, Catania and Siracusa. At the crossing from Villa San Giovanni on the Italian peninsula the train carriages are shunted into the ferry, and then shunted off again Messina. Palermo's main station Stazione Centrale. Always book a se for long-distance travel.

For information and online boo ing visit the Trenitalia website (ww trenitalia.com) or call tel: 892021 (t number, expect long waits). Ticke can be picked up (or bought direct from one of the self-service machine at the station.

Arriving by sea

A regular ferry and catamaran servic is run by Virtu Ferries (www.virtufe ries.com) from Catania and Pozzal to Malta. A number of ferries fro other Mediterranean ports, includin Citavecchia, Genoa, Livorno, Salern and Palermo run regularly. Visit www ferriesmalta.com for more informa tion on times and services.

Arriving by car

As aforementioned, there are no dire roads linking Malta to Europe, how ever you may drive to mainland Ita from various parts in Europe, inclu ing the UK, and get a ferry to Malta.

Driving to Sicily from the UK take around 24 hours. Even from Rom it is a good seven hours to Villa Sa Giovanni in Calabria, where you cros to Sicily. To bring a car into Malta yo will need a current driving licenc and valid insurance. You must carr your driving licence, car registratio insurance documents and passpor

Tallinja Cards offer unlimited travel for seven days

with you at all times when driving. You are also required to carry a triangular warning sign and a high visibility vest.

Transport around Malta

Driving

A car in Malta can help you get around much more easily than when using public transport, which can be relatively unreliable. Be aware that, just like in England and some other countries around the world, people in Malta drive on the left-hand side.

Most roads are in decent condition, although you may find potholes even in main roads. Traffic jams are one of the main problems currently affecting the island, so plan well-ahead if you need to be somewhere on time.

Car hire

Most international car hire companies have a branch in Malta, including Avis (www.avis.com.mt) and Budget (www.budget.com.mt). Other companies based solely in Malta exist as well, and you'll find them on www.yellow.com.mt. In Malta you need to be at least 21 years of age to be eligible to rent a car, with a Younger Driver Surcharge applicable for drivers under 25. A clean driving licence held for at least 12 months in your country of residence is a requirement for most car hiring companies.

Rules and regulations

Like the UK, driving in Malta takes place on the left-hand side of the road, and it's particularly important to keep this in mind when approaching a roundabout. Drivers already encircling a roundabout always have right of way. Overtaking is acceptable but make sure you check what your fellow drivers are up to before you do so. Limits are of 80km/h on open roads, with 50km/h in built-up areas, yet these change depending on the area and signs signalling the top speed for that road are ubiquitous. It is illegal to not wear a seat belt, even in the back.

Parking

Expect to spend at least 10 minutes looking for a parking space wherever you go, and that includes some privately-owned car parks, too. Parking metres are not common, but you'll find some in Sliema and Valletta. When in Valletta, you will notice different coloured parking bays as part of the Valletta Control Vehicular Access System (CVA). White parking bays are for both residents and non-residents and available 24-hours a day; green parking bays are for residents only and available to them 24 hours a day; blue parking bays are available to non-residents between 8am and 6pm daily.

Fuel

Petrol is readily available at many 24-hour stations with self-service dispensers that accept euro notes and credit cards, though it's wise to always bring cash in case the credit card machine is out of order. Please note, that fuel prices in Malta are

much higher than the average in Europe.

Rail

The only two modes of transport available on the island are on-land vehicles (private cars, buses and taxis) and water ferries. No railways or trams operate on Malta, Gozo or Comino.

Taxi

Licenced taxis are white, and they are available at most big cities, particularly outside Valletta, Mdina, in Sliema, St Julian's and Cirkewwa. Although the meter is sometimes used, it is custom to agree the fee before heading off to your desired destination. White taxis tend to be more expensive than taxis operating as part of a company. Airport taxis need to be booked from the designated stand at Arrivals.

For reliable companies offering taxi service, visit www.yellow.com.mt. Some of Malta's top taxi services include:

eCabs, Triq Elija Zammit, San Giljan; tel: 2138 3838; www.ecabs.com.mt

John's Group, Triq Elija Zammit, San Giljan; tel: 2298 2298; https://johns cabsmalta.business.site

Wembley Motors, 115, Triq San Gorg, San Giljan; tel: 2137 4141; www.wembleys.com

Greenr cabs, Birkirkara; tel: 2738 3838; www.greenr.cab

Bus

Malta's bus service runs daily between approximately 5.30am and 11pm; and night buses operate in some areas from 11pm onwards. There are over 80 routes to and from various hubs that connect the island. Tickets cost €2 for a single journey in summer, €1.50 in winter; and €3 at night – these can be purchased directly on the bus. A 'tallinja card explore' at €21 for adults and €15 for children offers seven days of unlimited travel including night services; while a €15 tallinja card will get you 12 single day journeys. These can be bought from the Malta Public Transport office near the bus hub outside Valletta. For more information, visit www.tallinja.com.

Ferry

Gozo Channel has a frequent ferry service running daily to and from Gozo on an almost hourly basis, including at night. The trip takes between 20–30 minutes depending on many variables, including the wind. Standard passenger rate is €4.65 during the day and €4.05 at night; children cost €1.15. Car and driver fare is €15.70 during the day and €12.80 at night; all other passengers on board the car pay normal fares. The rates are inclusive of return, and they are paid in full on the way back from Gozo to Malta. For summer and winter timetables, as well as fares for bicycles and motorcycle and driver, visit www.gozochannel.com.

Ferries from Valletta to Sliema and the Three Cities (Cospicua, Senglea and Vittoriosa) are also run on a daily basis, and they are the fastest way to get your destination. An adult single

A classic car in mint condition

ticket costs €1.50, while return costs €2.80; children pay €0.50 for single and €0.90 for return. These cannot be paid for using the afore-mentioned tallinja card. For information on summer and winter timetables, visit www.vallettaferryservices.com.

Please see 'Arriving by sea' for information on visiting Sicily by ferry.

Segway

Segways have become a popular mode of transport in Malta. While they haven't yet made it onto the busy roads, they are to be found whizzing through many towns and villages, including Valletta and Mdina. Even members of the local police force can sometimes be seen patrolling on the two-wheelers.

A Segway tour will certainly give you a different perspective of the island, and it's a fun way to spend an afternoon, or even a full day. Popular tours include the Dingli-to-Buskett route, which makes the most of the sweeping view of this island's most dramatic cliffscape. The Gozo tour is also great fun, and makes light work of the island's hilly terrain as you zoom through the country lanes and villages, stopping en route for a piping-hot slice of local pizza.

Visas and passports

Visas for visitors from EU countries are not required, with a current passport or valid ID being sufficient. For visitors from the US, Canada, Australia or New Zealand a visa is not required, but a valid e-passport is essential for entry to be granted for a stay of up to three months. For a list of nationalities that require a visa, visit http://homeaffairs.gov.mt. Visas must be obtained in advance from a Maltese Embassy or Consulate. Malta is part of Schengen, and persons allowed to enter the country are free to roam Schengen states for 90 days.

Weights and measures

Both the Metric and the Imperial Systems are used on the Maltese Islands, with the Metric System being the more popular one.

Women travellers

Women in Malta enjoy equal rights on all fronts, and it is perfectly safe for women to travel alone. Cases of serious harassment and sexual assaults are rare, but it is advisable for them to be with a friend when going to clubs or bars, particularly in Paceville, St Julian's. Both men and women are advised to keep an eye on their drink when out on the town, not to give their personal details to strangers, and to inform a friend if they are leaving with someone who they may not know well.

Most policemen speak English

LANGUAGE

Mati, or Maltese, is spoken daily in Malta and Gozo. It is a language that dates back more than 1,000 years with roots that go back to Phoenician and Carthaginian times, and has a solid base in Arabic. Over the years, words from various other languages, including Italian, French and English have infiltrated the language and, today, it is the only Semitic language in the world written in Latin font.

English is an official language of the Republic of Malta, and most people on Malta and Gozo can speak English fluently. Even so, knowing and using basic Maltese words in conversation will be appreciated by the islanders and will help you to pronounce place names properly.

General

Goog morning bongu
Good evening bonswa
Goodbye sahha
How are you? kif int?
Yes Iva
No Le
Thank you Grazzi
You're Welcome Ta' xejn
Please Jekk joghgbok
Excuse me (to get attention) Skużani
Excuse me (in a crowd) Skużi
Could you help me? Tista' tghini?
Certainly Mela le
Can you show me (where)...? Tista'

turini (fejn)...?
I need... Ghandi bżonn...
I'm lost Intlift
I'm sorry Skużani
I don't know Ma nafx
I don't understand Mhux qed nifhem
Do you speak English/French/ Spanish? Titkellem Ingliż/Franciż/ Spanjol?
Could you speak more slowly? Jimporta titkellem aktar bil-mod?
Could you repeat that please? Jimporta terga' tirrepeti x'ghadek kif ghidtdli, jekk joghgbok?
How much does it cost? Kemm tiswa'?
this one/that one Din/Dik (f.) or Dan/Dak (m.)
Have you got...? Ghandek...?

At a bar/restaurant

I'd like to book a table Nixtieq nirriżerva mejda
Have you got a table for... Ghandkom mejda ghall-...
I have a reservation Ibbukjajt
lunch l-ikla ta' wara nofsinhar
supper l-ikla ta' filghaxija
I'm vegetarian Jien vegetarjan/a
May we have the menu? Jimporta ggibilna l-menu, jekk joghgbok?
What would you like? X'tixtieq tiehu?
I'd like... Jien ha niehu...
mineral water ilma
fizzy/still bil-gas/still

PALACE SQUARE
MISRAH IL-PALAZZ

Bilingual sign

a bottle of flixkun
a glass of tazza
red wine inbid ahmar
white wine inbid abjad
beer birra

Numbers

One Wiehed
Two Tnejn
Three Tlieta
Four Erbgha
Five Hamsa
Six Sitta
Seven Sebgha
Eight Tmienja
Nine Disgha
Ten Ghaxra
Twenty Ghoxrin
Thirty Tletin
Forty Erbghin
Fifty Hamsin
One Hundred Mijja
One Thousand Elf

Getting around

What time do you open/close? Fi x'hin tifthu/taghlqu?
Where can I buy tickets? Minnfejn nista' nixtri l-biljetti?
What time does the bus leave? Fi x'hin titlaq tal-linja?
Can you tell me where to get off? Jimporta tghidli fejn irrid nieqaf?
Where is the nearest bank/hotel? Fejn qieghed l-eqreb bank? Fejn qegh-dha l-eqreb hotel?
On the right Fuq il-lemin
On the left Fuq ix-xellug

Go straight on Ibqa' sejjer dritt

Online

Where's an Internet café? Hawn Internet café fil-vicinanzi?
Does it have wireness Internet? Ghandhom Wi-Fi?
What is the Wi-Fi password? X'inhi l-password tal-Wi-Fi?
Is the Wi-Fi free? Il-Wi-Fi b'xejn?
How do I turn the computer on/off? Kif nixghel/nitfi l-kompjuter?
Can I...? Nista'...?
access the Internet? nid ol onlajn?
check e-mail niccekja l-e-mails?
Print nipprintja
plug in/charge my laptop/iPhone/iPad? inqabbad/niccargja l-laptop/iPhone/iPad?
Access Skype? naccessa Skype?
How much per hour/half hour? Kemm ghal siegha/nofs siegha?
How do I...? Kif...?
connent/disconnent nikkonnektja/niddiskonnektja
log on/log off nidfhol fil/nohrog minn
What's your e-mail? X'inhu l-e-mail address tieghek?
My e-mail is... L-e-mail tieghi huwa...

Social media
Are you on Facebook/Twitter? Ghandek Facebook/Twitter?
What's your user name? X'inhu l-us-ername tieghek?
I'll add you as a friend. Issa naddjak.
I'll put the pictures on Facebook Ser intella r-ritratti fuq Facebook.

BOOKS AND FILM

Malta's history has shaped its representation in literature and film, creating a real mystique around it. From the Knights of St John, who were closely related to the Templars, to Malta's crucial role during World War II, the island is surrounded by legends and myths.

Malta is also a cinematographer's dream location with its picturesque seascapes and rough cliffs; no wonder it has served as the backdrop to some of Hollywood's biggest productions. Locally, the cinematographic scene is still in its infancy, yet award-winning film *Shimshar*, directed by local director Rebecca Cremona, has launched Malta onto the international cinema scene.

Books

The Story of Malta, by Maturin Murray Ballou, is a guide to Malta's history up until 1893: its early inhabitants and series of invasions from the Phoenicians to the British.

The Kapillan of Malta, by Nicholas Monsarrat, is a classic novel set in the second Great Siege of Malta (1940–1942). Ranking among the most famous literary works Malta has ever produced, this is the story of a fictional priest serving the poor of Valletta on the advent of World War II.

The Great Siege, by Ernle Bradford, tells the story of Malta during the time of the Great Siege of 1565, and how Sulei-

man the Magnificent was determined to conquer Europe.

The Sword and the Scimitar, by Simon Scarrow, brings the Great Siege of Malta to life in a stand-alone novel that recounts the ferocious attack by the Ottomans on Malta.

Memento Mori, by Dane Munro, offers a unique insight into the thoughts, fears and aspirations of the Knights of St John through the painstakingly-translated inscriptions on the tombstones inside St John's Co-Cathedral. It also has incredible photos of the floor of the Cathedral.

My Century, by Dr Michael A. Refalo, is a translation of Herbert Ganado's memoirs, *Rajt Malta Tinbidel*. As a Maltese lawyer, president of Catholic Action, editor, politician and author, Ganado experienced Malta under the British, was there when the island became an independent nation state, and was in the thick of it all when a civil war almost broke out in the late 1970s and early 80s.

Memories, by Peter Apap Bologna, is a three-part autobiography. From a childhood spent in a war-torn Malta, to being present at the official Independence Day celebrations, to witnessing the opening of the island's first art gallery, the author recounts how the past few decades affected the island and his life.

The Malta Story

A Taste of History: The Food of the Knights of Malta, by Pamela Parkinson-Large, takes readers on a tour of the food enjoyed by the people of Malta hundreds of years ago. This also narrates the story of how the country's cuisine was influenced by countries from as far afield as North Africa and the Holy Land.

Malta: The Medieval Millennium, by Charles Dalli, tells the story of Malta from the end of the Roman rule to the arrival of the Knights Hospitallers.

Malta's Barriers of Beauty, by world-renowned fine arts photographer Brett B Field, is a photographic journey documenting the artistic and enchanting doors of Malta.

The International Dictory of Artists Who Painted Malta, by Marquis Nicholas de Piro, is an anthology of paintings about the Maltese Islands.

Costume in Malta – A History of Fabric Form & Fashion, by Marquis Nicholas de Piro, is a highly-researched publication of historical dress, fashion, styles and accessories from all echelons of Maltese society.

Films

The Malta Story (1953) is a British war film based on the heroic air defence of Malta during the Siege of Malta in World War II. The film includes unique footage of the locations at which the battles were actually fought.

Simshar (2014) was the first Maltese film to be nominated for an Academy Award for Best Foreign Language. The film is based on the true story of the 'Simshar', a fishing boat which sank in the waters between Malta and Africa – a story which shook Malta to its core.

The Maltese Falcon (1941) is a film noir starring Humphrey Bogart and Mary Astor. The story revolves around three eccentric criminals and their quest for a priceless statuette, which, in 1539, was sent to King Charles V of Spain by the Knights Templars of Malta to pay tribute.

The Siege of Malta: The George Cross Island (2014) is a documentary about the Siege of Malta during World War II. The documentary contains unseen wartime footage, as well as interviews from some of the heroic survivors.

Munich (2005) was directed by Steven Spielberg and shot in Malta, Budapest, Paris and New York. The film features scenes shot in Valletta, Sliema, Bugibba, Marsaxlokk, Cospicua, Marsa, Rabat and at Malta International Airport.

Captain Phillips (2013) starred Tom Hanks as the title character and was inspired by the 2009 Maersk Alabama pirate hijacking. It was nominated for Best Picture in 2014.

Murder on the Orient Express (2017) based on the Agatha Christie novel starring Penélope Cruz, Willem Dafoe, Judi Dench, and Johnny Depp. Some scenes were filmed in Valletta, among other destinations in Europe.

ABOUT THIS BOOK

This *Explore Guide* has been produced by the editors of Insight Guides, whose books have set the standard for visual travel guides since 1970. With top-quality photography and authoritative recommendations, these guidebooks bring you the very best routes and itineraries in the world's most exciting destinations.

BEST ROUTES

The routes in the book provide something to suit all budgets, tastes and trip lengths. As well as covering the destination's many classic attractions, the itineraries track lesser-known sights. The routes embrace a range of interests, so whether you are an art fan, a gourmet, a history buff or have kids to entertain, you will find an option to suit.

We recommend reading the whole of a route before setting out. This should help you to familiarise yourself with it and enable you to plan where to stop for refreshments – options are shown in the 'Food and Drink' box at the end of each tour.

For our pick of the tours by theme, consult Recommended Routes for... (see pages 6–7).

INTRODUCTION

The routes are set in context by this introductory section, giving an overview of the destination to set the scene, plus background information on food and drink, shopping and more, while a succinct history timeline highlights the key events over the centuries.

DIRECTORY

Also supporting the routes is a Directory chapter, with a clearly organised A–Z of practical information, our pick of where to stay while you are there and select restaurant listings; these eateries complement the more low-key cafés and restaurants that feature within the routes and are intended to offer a wider choice for evening dining. Also included here are some nightlife listings, plus a handy language guide and our recommendations for books and films about the destination.

ABOUT THE AUTHORS

Jo Caruana is a British-born writer but has lived in Malta for most of her life. She runs content company Writemeanything and corporate etiquette consultancy Finesse, while also writing for local and foreign travel publications.

CONTACT THE EDITORS

We hope you find this Explore Guide useful, interesting and a pleasure to read. If you have any questions or feedback on the text, pictures or maps, please do let us know. If you have noticed any errors or outdated facts, or have suggestions for places to include on the routes, we would be delighted to hear from you. Please drop us an email at hello@insightguides.com. Thanks!

CREDITS

Explore Malta
Editor: Sian Marsh
Author: Jo Caruana
Head of DTP and Pre-Press: Rebeka Davies
Update Production: Apa Digital
Picture Editors: Tom Smyth & Aude Vauconsant
Cartography: Carte
Photo credits: Alamy 4MC, 10, 28ML, 80/81; Barracuda 4MC; Denise Wilkins/ 81L; Essence 100; Getty Images 1, 4/5T, 27, 60/61, 105; Hilton Hotels & Resorts 96; Infinitely Xara 17L; iStock 24, 30/31, 40, 73L, 82/83, 84MC, 112, 115, 118; Leonardo 86; Level 22 103; Mike Watson Photography/viewingmalta.com 41; MTA/ Mario Galea 13; Photoshot 120, 121; Shutterstock 39, 42/43, 52, 68/69, 72, 75, 108; Sylvaine Poitau/Apa Publications 4ML, 4MR, 6BC, 7T, 8MC, 8/9T, 11, 12, 19, 28MR, 28ML, 28MR, 32, 33, 35, 36, 36/37, 44, 47L, 49, 50, 51B, 53, 55T, 56/57, 57L, 62/63, 65T, 66, 70, 71L, 70/71, 72/73, 74, 76, 77, 78, 79, 80, 84ML, 94, 95, 101, 106, 107, 109, 110, 111, 112B, 113, 114, 116, 117, 119; Teatru Aurora 8ML; Viewing Malta 4ML, 4MR, 6MC, 6TL, 6ML, 7M, 7MR, 7MR, 8ML, 8MC, 8MR, 8MR, 14/15, 16, 16/17, 18, 20, 20/21, 21L, 22, 23, 25, 26, 28MC, 28MC, 28/29T, 34, 37L, 38, 45, 46, 46/47, 48, 51T, 54, 55B, 56, 58, 59, 62, 63L, 64, 65B, 67, 70B, 84ML, 84MR, 84MR, 84MC, 84/85T, 87, 88, 89, 90, 91, 92, 93, 97, 98, 99, 102, 104
Cover credits: Getty Images (main) iStock (bottom)

Printed by CTPS – China

Second Edition 2019

DISTRIBUTION

UK, Ireland and Europe
Apa Publications (UK) Ltd
sales@insightguides.com
United States and Canada
Ingram Publisher Services
ips@ingramcontent.com
Australia and New Zealand
Woodslane
info@woodslane.com.au
Southeast Asia
Apa Publications (Singapore) Pte
singaporeoffice@insightguides.com
Worldwide
Apa Publications (UK) Ltd
sales@insightguides.com

SPECIAL SALES, CONTENT LICENSING AND COPUBLISHING

Insight Guides can be purchased in bulk quantities at discounted prices. We can create special editions, personalised jackets and corporate imprints tailored to your needs.
sales@insightguides.com
www.insightguides.biz

INDEX

MAP LEGEND

- ●   Start of tour
- →   Tour & route direction
- ❶   Recommended sight
- ❷   Recommended restaurant/café
- ★   Place of interest
- ❶   Tourist information
- ✉   Post office
- ⚊   Statue/monument
-   Tower
- ⋒   Museum/gallery
- 📖   Library
- 🎭   Theatre

- ✚   Hospital
- ✿   Police
- ⛪   Church
-   Chapel
-   Monastery
- ☪   Mosque
- 🚌   Main bus station
- 🅿   Car park
- ✈   International airport
- ⚓   Harbour
-   Castle
-   Lighthouse
-   Windmill
-   Beach

-   Cave
-   Dolmen
- ⁝   Ancient site
- ✳   Viewpoint
-   Golf/Tennis
-   Yachting
-   Windsurfing
-   Water skiing
-   Scuba diving
-   Fishing
-   Park
-   Important building
-   Urban area
-   Non-urban area
- † †   Cemetery

INSIGHT  GUIDES

OFF THE SHELF

Since 1970, INSIGHT GUIDES has provided a unique perspective on the world's best travel destinations by using specially commissioned photography and illuminating text written by local authors.

Whether you're planning a city break, a walking tour or the journey of a lifetime, our superb range of guidebooks and phrasebooks will inspire you to discover more about your chosen destination.

INSIGHT GUIDES

offer a unique combination of stunning photos, absorbing narrative and detailed maps, providing all the inspiration and information you need.

CITY GUIDES

pack hundreds of great photos into a smaller format with detailed practical information, so you can navigate the world's top cities with confidence.

POCKET GUIDES

combine concise information on where to go and what to do in a handy compact format, ideal on the ground. Includes a full-colour, fold-out map.

EXPERIENCE GUIDES

feature offbeat perspectives and secret gems for experienced travellers, with a collection of over 100 ideas for a memorable stay in a city.

www.insightguides.com